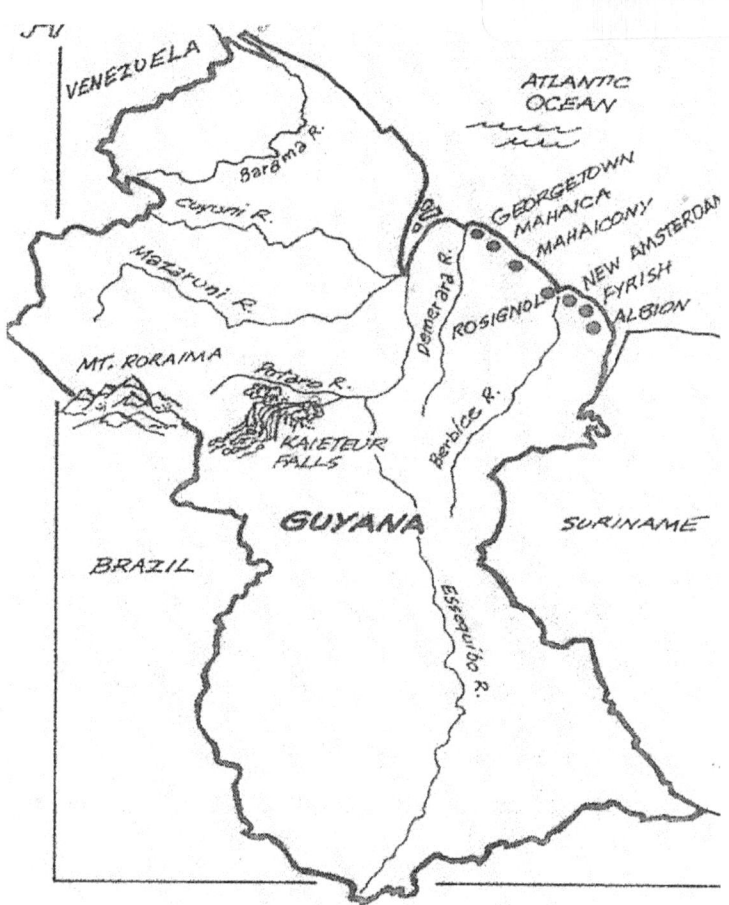

Map of Guyana showing Albion Estate

A Journey across the Oceans In Search for Lost Love

An Indo-Guyanese Experience

by

HARRY RICKHEERAM

Copyright © 2015 by Harry Rickheeram
Printed in the United States.
All rights reserved
No part of this book may be reproduced or transmitted in any form or by electronic, mechanical, photocopying, recording or otherwise without written permission of the author. All names and characters are fictitious and bear no resemblances to anyone living or dead.

ISBN: 0-9723647-7-3

Library of Congress Control Number: 2015918487

Compiled by Palm Tree Enterprises
Mount Dora, Florida
352-735-2730

Acknowledgments

Many people have contributed to the writing of this book in one form or another, and I am pleased to acknowledge a few of them.

Special thanks to my brother **Mootiram Rickheeram** for his contribution and encouragement in writing and publishing this book.

Thanks also to **Bruce Cooper**, **Morris Sankar, Savitree Pohal, Rachel Rupsingh, Mya Rickheeram** and my uncle **Joseph Persaud.**

Dedication

I dedicate this book to all my ancestors who made the sacrifice and traveled thousands of miles across the *kala pani* from their native India to British Guiana, hoping to make a better life for their family. Instead, they found themselves indentured and were forced to give their tears, sweat, blood and lives to the cruel and greedy, aristocratic sugar plantation owners who lorded over them. They endured the suffering meted out to them throughout Indentured Servitude, longing to finish their terms of indenture and buy a piece of land and exist independently, or return home to India penniless.

Those who stayed, including my grandparents, achieved their dreams and unshackled themselves from the cruel yolk of imperialism. It took nearly three decades to accomplish this without abandoning their Hindu customs and traditions, but the younger generation had difficulty blending Eastern thoughts with Western customs. Today, girls are allowed to attend school and the old timers no longer demand the custom of arranged marriages.

Our foreparents, unfortunately, are not here to enjoy the fruits of what they sought when they first came to this land. Our lives are indeed better than those who were left behind in the remote villages of India which remain almost the same today as before our ancestors left.

Special dedication goes to my great-great-grand parents, **Ramgolam** and **Rukmin** who took the risk and traveled from the remote Village of Utter Pradesh with their children **Deowkey, Chunilall, Sookram**, and also my great-grand mother **Ratnie** who later married **Mohabir**, an immigrant from a small Village in Behar. Also to my mom, **Budhni**, my dad, **Rickheeram** and other family members: **Bharrat, Lachia, Jaharie (aka Surania), Jesodra (aka Bobby), Chan**,

***Girdharry*, Samdarie. Ramrattan, Sahodrie, Tarasia, Gigri, Mangru, Annie, Baichan** and **Basmattie.**

Special dedication also goes to *Joseph Persaud* (aka *Senarine*), the oldest surviving member of our descendants and at ninety-three years old he advised and guided me through the process of book writing; and to my mom **Budhni Rickheeram** (aka *Janie*) who passed away at age ninety. She gave me the inspiration to write this book after witnessing the struggle she encountered as an early Indian female descendant, who was caught between the Eastern and Western Cultures that still exist during my life as a third generation Indo-Guyanese. I am happy today finally to witness the cultural changes that have now taken place for my children, grand children and future generations.

Contents

Introduction
My early life
Meeting my best friend
My first date
Going to High School
My Last Year as a Teenager
Death of my father
In search of my Uncle
My first job in Trinidad
Working in the sugar-cane fields
My job as a supervisor
Monica's return trip to British Guiana
The death of Rohan
My first trip to United States
Raj departed to College
Sharmila's vacation in Trinidad
My trip to British Guiana
Ram's Retirement
Major Announcement
Sharmila and Raj learned the truth
Trip to India
My marriage celebration
Conclusion

Introduction

The story of "*Across the Oceans—In search for lost love*" is set in the early nineteen hundreds and travels across four countries on four different continents—India (Asia), British Guiana (South America), Trinidad (Central America), and the United States (North America).

It relates to the hardships and miseries many of the youths who were descendants of indentured East Indians endured growing up in poverty in a Third World country, sharing values that conflicted with those of their ancestors who migrated there from India.

This book is based on family values, tragedies, strict Hindu cultures and customs that were forced upon a generation growing up in a different era. It is about love, separation, family disputes when riches clashed with poverty and the struggles we faced trying to mesh Eastern with Western cultures. It tells about some of the hard times youths endured, and some of the good times they enjoyed. It also describes the struggle and hardship they encountered when they fell in love.

It's a love story about a poor boy who grew up in a little known third world country and fell in love with his childhood girl friend, thus undermining the strict rules of his Indian immigrant parents whose cultures forbid youths from courting and falling in love. Their parents strongly believed in arranged marriages—a belief that most of the time, resulted in many broken hearts and even suicides. It is often a fierce struggle as Indo-Guianese children struggle as they try to follow the strict Indian cultures, customs and religion while at the same time trying to cope with the western cultures that surround them all the time.

Chapter 1
My early life

My life began in a small, Third World country called British Guiana, which is now known as The Republic of Guyana. It is located in the Northeastern section of the continent of South America. I was born and raised there and known by the name Ricky.

While growing up in poverty, there were many obstacles that I encountered and had to endure and overcome, especially when I fell in love and made the sacrifice to be with the one that I truly loved. There were many tragedies and also some triumphs during my quest to gain my love that led me to believe that the word "Love" cannot be explained in its true meaning unless one experienced and felt the joy and pain to discover it.

I recall growing up as a little boy in this small countryside Village in the Eastern section of British Guiana. I was told that my ancestors came to this Village as immigrant laborers after slavery was abolished. My parents along with other Indians were brought to replace the slaves in the sugar industry, and they brought with them their strict customs and cultures which led to many broken hearts for the younger generation that were born in a different era and I was no exception.

I grew up in a "cottage like" home, identified as *logies* by the plantation owners. These were the original housing for the slaves. When I was only five years old, I experienced the first major tragedy of my life. I cannot forget that day when my mother got sick with pneumonia and because there were little medical facilities available to help her, she suffered in bed with breathing problems and unable to walk for a period of approximately three months, as my dad took care of her before she finally passed away. At that time, I was not old enough to understand *Life and Death* but I knew the one whom I loved dearly will not be around to cherish and cuddle me anymore with that loving touch which she gave me as a child while I was growing up. I was heartbroken as she was taken and buried in a small cemetery beside the sugarcane fields that are now lost forever because of neglect by the estate management.

I still remember my mother's charming and tender touch as she helped me while doing her day-to-day chores. Unfortunately during those days no one took pictures, so the only thing to remind me of such a wonderful woman was my faint memory of her beautiful face which always had a loving smile as she spoke with her soft melodious voice, and her silky long hair as it swayed from side to side as she walked. She was such a pretty woman.

After my mother's death my father became both my father and my mother. He worked in the sugar fields cutting sugar cane from morning till night, toiling for a meagre salary, which was barely enough to provide for our daily meals. Each day after a hard day's work in the sugar cane field, my father came home in the afternoon and prepared our meals for dinner. He got up at 4:00 o'clock in the morning and prepared our breakfast and lunch before heading to work.

My father was very popular and well known in the Village. He was light brown in complexion; medium built about 5ft. 8in. in height. He was very loving but strict and was born in the highest cast according to the Indian religious belief. He was a *Brahmin,* which class is considered in India as a leader and a teacher. Even in Guiana during that period the Indian immigrants respected my father and asked for his advice and guidance whenever needed.

I recall that every afternoon on his way from work, my father would buy a quarter bottle of rum, which he drank before his dinner to calm his tired body and aching bones.

My father's favorite meal for dinner was yellow split peas (*dahl*) and rotie. In the morning he always ate *sada rotie* (pita bread) mixed with onions and pepper. He also had fried vegetables and potatoes with rice for his lunch. During that period there were not many means of transportation. Most people including my father walked many miles each day to and from the cane-fields where they toiled the entire day. The managers of the estate rode mules to the fields.

The immigrant Indians lived in broken down cottages, which were the original housing for the Negro slaves who preceded them. The cottages were about 100ft. long with either wooden or mud walls and divided into sections, each section with one room and one window. Family space was about ten feet wide with an added extension in the back and it had a wood stove, (meaning a stove that is fired by wood) made of mud and called a *chulha*. This was our kitchen and this was where we cooked our food. There was no family privacy; neighbors next door could hear every conversation coming from the rooms nearby. We lived in a section of the cottage located on the western side of the settlement, and we had only one bedroom that was shared by my father and me. There was no bed, so we slept on the floor, with no sheets to cover or pillows. We were accustomed to sleeping on this hard surface. I must also admit that we were not the only ones, but most of the settlement-residents lived under the same condition as us.

There were no toilets on the properties of the cottages. Residents used toilets that were located over the trench that was built at the back of the settlement. These toilets were shaped like small houses and were divided into sections with a hole cut out at the center that was used as toilets. Passing by, one could hear the sound of excrement splashing into the water.

As a child growing up in poverty, I did not have many clothes, so the ones that I had were patched over and over when torn. I had two new shirts and two new pants that I always kept neatly folded and placed on a shelf that was in our bedroom. I used those new clothes only for special occasions. During that period everyone including myself, walked bare feet (no shoes). The soles of our feet became harder as we grew older and did not hurt as we walked on hard surfaces and the hot sandy roads.

I had many chores since I was a small boy. I cleaned and swept the house, washed the utensils, fetched water from the canals for both washing and drinking. I washed our clothes at the canal and fetched wood from the farms for cooking. A toothbrush was considered a luxury and only the rich could afford to buy one. We used special pieces of wood that were cut from the black-sage bush. The wood was then cut into pieces, about four inches in length, with one end chewed to form a brush, which was then used to brush our teeth. Also, toothpaste was a luxury so we used salt instead of paste.

During that period, there was no electricity. We lit lamps to get light. Since most of us could not afford to buy lamps, we made our own lamps by filling bottles with kerosene oil, made wicks with pieces of old cloth and sealed the heads with clay. There was no stove for cooking; as I previously mentioned we made wood-burning stoves with clay, which had one or two holes at the top for the pots and one hole at the front and center to place the wood. This is called a *fireside or chulha.* We used a piece of pipe 10 to 12 inches in length, to blow air in the *fireside* to help light the wood. We also used a flat round steel, called *tawa,* on which we cooked a home-made flatbread called *rotie*.

Most Guianese could not afford to buy plates or cups, so they used a substitute called *calabash.* It's made from a fruit that is shaped like a coconut and has a soft white crust inside. It grows on a calabash tree. To make bowls, the fruit is sawed in half and the inside is scraped out, leaving only the casing, which was referred to as the shell. The shells are then dried in the sun until they become hardened. When they are hardened, they are used as eating and washing utensils.

The *calabash* fruit can also be made into a *goblet* which was used for storing water. The *goblet* is made by cutting a round hole, about two inches in diameter, on one end of the *calabash*. The inside is then scraped clean, leaving only the casing. The casing is then dried and, when it is dry and hard, it becomes a goblet. Drinking water, which keeps cool, is stored in it.

When I was about eight years old, my father managed to save enough money generated from selling our farm produce to buy cows and sheep, which gave me some more responsibilities in taking care of the cattle. I took them to the pasture in the morning and brought them back in the evening. My father cut some grass for them on his way back from work.

One incident that I vaguely remembered when I went to the pasture to get our cattle, there was a wild bull. Unaware that this bull was wild, I walked beside him. All of a sudden he charged fiercely towards me. I ran, jumping over some bushes and puddles of water on my way as I tried to escape. I could not outrun the fierce bull and in one instance, he caught me before I could escape, and rammed its head onto my back throwing me to the ground. As I lay motionless the bull circled around me a few times before leaving. Thank god I was not hit by the bull's horns and I only suffered some bumps and bruises. My dad applied some hot water and then some warm coconut oil to the affected area and gave me some local medicine to drink.

Although I was just a small boy, I assisted my father with many chores that were done by adults. Today I am very happy that I did all of those things because it made me stronger and gave me the knowledge to prepare me for my future. It gave me the skills and ambition to do better in my life and forced me to do better for myself.

My childhood best friend while growing up was a boy named Jayboy. I could always count on him for help whenever I needed it. We hungout together, played games and visited each other homes frequently. Later in life both of us fell in love with girls (Monica and Sharda) who were also our best childhood friends.

Chapter 2
Meeting my best friend

When I was about nine years old, my dad managed to save enough money to purchase a property in a neighboring village called Kilcoy Settlement, which was a newly built section on the western section of the sugar estate. Most of the houses were single family, built on stilts (posts) about eight to nine feet in height. The bottom section, which we called the *bottom house,* was open and we used it for playing.

At my new residence, I met some other neighborhood kids, Ramesh and Sharda, who became my friends. Jayboy also spent most of the days with us.

I continued to attend primary school, which I started to attend since I was seven years old. The school was located in the eastern end of the estate about a mile from our house. The name of the school was Albion C.M Primary School, which was owned by the Christian Missionary Church but administered by the British government. The school curriculum was strictly British. We celebrated Christmas and Easter holidays. We sang the British national anthem every morning before classes started, and also saluted the Union Jack. Before the first period each morning, we received biscuits, milk and cod liver oil capsules. Sometimes, I did not swallow my capsules, but hid them under my tongue, and then I spat them out in the garbage bin when no one was looking.

While growing up, I was very shy and quiet, but I was a good student. I received certificates for regular attendance and for good behavior almost every year.

Going to school, then, was so different than from today. Teachers, in those days, were allowed to inflict corporal punishment on students who misbehaved and who did not answer all the test questions correctly, especially in arithmetic and dictation. Each mistake earned one lash with a cane provided by the Ministry of Education.

I remember one day during lunch break, my friends and I went to a nearby sugar-cane field to steal sugar cane. One of the estate managers saw us and chased us. We ran and managed to hide in the nearby bushes and waited until the manager left then went back to school. To our surprise, the manager was waiting at the school with the principal. The manager identified one of my friends, and he was taken into the principal's office. My friend gave us all up and we were called to the office. We were then thrown over the desk by the principal and each one of us received six lashes on the buttocks. Some kids wore double pants just in case they received this sort of punishment.

Another incident I encountered at school was one day when we were in the auditorium and some students were misbehaving, throwing things at each other. The teacher, Mr. Singh came in unexpectedly, ran after us, whipping the students that were caught. While running away, I fell and bruised my arm as the students ran over me as they tried to escape the teacher's whipping. My father saw the marks on my arm and questioned me about it; but before I could answer, my friend Jayboy who was at my house at the time told my dad about the incident. My dad became very furious and went to the school. He wanted to assault Mr. Singh, the teacher, because he was told by one of the students that the teacher, which caused the marks on my arm, beat me. But the principal explained to my father what actually occurred, and he eventually calmed down.

While in primary school, I got into a lot of other mischievous things with my friend Jayboy. We enjoyed stealing our neighbor's ginnips, guavas and mangoes. I remember some days we went to the farm after school. We cut a few bunches of bananas, hid them in the bushes to ripen, we did that at least three times per week and we were never in short of ripe bananas which we snacked on every afternoon after school.

Another incident I cannot forget is when I went with Jayboy to visit his cousin after school at Fyrish, our neighboring Village, I did the worst thing I can remember doing. We played games with Jayboy's cousin and were having fun, losing track of time. I always went home after school before my father came from work, except that day. To make matter worse while we were returning home, we were confronted by two of Jayboy's class mates. One of them had an argument with Jayboy earlier in the day at school and he brought his friend to take revenge. They started attacking Jayboy punching him throwing him to the ground. I tried to separate them, only to find myself being attacked. I had no alternative but to defend myself as I returned a few punches while Jayboy managed to get back on his feet and picked a piece of wood that he found by the side of the street, hitting the attackers as they ran for their lives.

Thank God Jayboy ended up only with slight bruises. I went home when it was almost dark. My father was angry and was waiting for me with a belt. For the first time my father gave me a good whipping until my skin was swollen. After he calmed down, he washed my wound, bathed me with water boiled with *neem* leaves, and rubbed some coconut oil on the wound. He then had a good talk with me. I also promised him that I would never do that again.

The following day, I could not go to school because I had a fever, and I was also in pain. I must also admit that during that period whipping like that was not considered abuse but was considered one of the ways of leading children in the right direction. I was not the only child who suffered this kind of punishment. If children were caught doing anything wrong, neighbors, friends or any member of the family, including uncles, aunts, had the authority to whip them; and if the children went home and complained, they got some more whipping from their parents.

At school, every morning during the first period, we did physical exercises; and, once yearly, we competed with other schools in *track and field*. I represented my school in the under- twelve 500-meters races the long jump, the bag race, the relay race, and the three-legged race. I was very physically active.

After school, other activities in which we participated, included racing, cricket, enter-hole, a game played with marbles. Some other games that we played were *Sal Pass* and hide-and-seek. Most days we played these games at Ramesh's home.

One of my most memorable days was while Jayboy and I were playing with Ramesh and his sister (Sharda) at their home, one of their next-door neighbors came over and joined us. I did not know that my entire future life would be changed from that day. This girl was so pretty that I could not stop staring at her and I found myself attracted to her. That was the first time I had laid eyes on Monica, whose name I had not known at the time. I was only ten years old and she was eight.

She was fair in complexion and had blue eyes. I thought that she was a perfect match for me to be my friend and probably my girl friend when I grew up. I always admired people with blue eyes and fair complexion. I believe my admiration was derived from seeing the British daily while growing up in the sugar estate. After Sharda introduced us, we played games for a long period of time as I kept staring at this girl's beauty as she smiled and I sometimes held her hand while playing.

As evening came, Monica's parents called her, telling her that it was time to come home for dinner. Before she left, I managed to ask her if she would be my friend and she replied "yes." That was the happiest day of my life.

I found out that Monica and I were attending the same school and I cannot forget the first time Monica and I walked to school being alone together. At first she was a little shy walking with me alone but somehow we managed to start a conversation with each other. After that day I looked forward to seeing and walking with her every morning and afternoon to and from school.

Each passing day, I was drawn closer and closer to Monica, and I looked forward to going to school and waiting for her so as to see this beautiful girl and her pretty face. Being in her company made me feel very happy. At that time, I did not understand what being in love felt like because I was not even a teenager, but I must admit, though, that a different feeling came over me, as if Monica and I had met in a different life.

While growing up as a young boy, as I mentioned previously, I was a very shy and quiet person. It was hard for me to make conversation with girls; so my conversations with Monica and other female students were just schoolmate discussions. It was also a coincidence that she started attending the same *Mandir* (Hindu church) that I attended; and many times, while in *Mandir,* Monica and I caught ourselves staring at each other from across the hall. Within a couple of weeks, we became very close friends and spent most of our times being together. Our friendship started innocently but every time we were around each other, an unexplained feeling came over me that I did not understand. I could see that her feelings were the same as mine.

Monica lived a block away from me, so I did not have to walk a long distance to see her. After many months, we developed a closer relationship with each other and as we got older our relationship started to develop into a more loving and bonding friendship. We looked forward to recess and lunch breaks at school so that we could hang out and play together along with Jayboy and Sharda who were also our best friends.

After about three years walking to and from school and spending most weekends with each other, I knew that my feelings for Monica were more than just friends. I believe I was in love with her. I could see it in her also that she had the same type of feelings for me. Unfortunately, I had about six more months to graduate from primary school, and I was thinking about how much I would miss her company walking to and from school daily after graduation. So one day I decided to let her know how I felt about her and I expressed my love to her. She also expressed her love for me. That was one of the happiest days in my life to know that she had the same feelings for me that I had for her.

I cannot forget the last day of school. She waited for me in the afternoon, and on our way back home I saw the tears in her eyes as we made a commitment to each other that we would be friends forever no matter what obstacles, came in our way, we would overcome them.

A few months later, Monica was no longer allowed to go out and play with friends after school or weekends because her parents felt that she was getting older; and as per their customs and cultures she was forbidden to be around boys at her age. So we decided that we would communicate with each other through letters. Monica arranged with her friend Sharda to be our messenger in delivering mails for us.

After Monica graduated from primary school, we hardly talked to each other; but during the day and evening, I passed by her house just to get a glimpse of her beautiful face and her loving smile as she looked for me from her window. I received my first letter two weeks after she finished school. I was very much overjoyed as I read all those loving words as she expressed her feelings for me. I responded to her letter also expressing my feelings and commitment to her. A few times when her parents were not home, she would sneak across to Sharda's house where Jayboy and I along with Sharda's brother would hang out and play games together.

I continued every evening to walk around Monica's house just to get a glimpse of her. During that period the strict Indian customs and culture were very much part of our lives. Teenage girls were not allowed to socialize with boys outside of their houses, so we looked at each other across the street smiling with each other.

Apart from spending time at Sharda's house, I was also involved in other activities such as playing cricket and volleyball. My dad later bought a bicycle for me which I enjoyed riding, and I suffered many injuries. In one incident, while competing in a bicycle race at the Chesney cricket ground, I fell on the curb and bruised my shoulder so badly that my shoulder bones were exposed. In another incident, while standing on a wedge on the back of my bicycle while my friend Jayboy was riding, my foot got caught in the spokes of the back wheel. A large piece of flesh on my calf got badly mangled, exposing the bones. To this day, the mark is still visible. Another time, while riding my bicycle to Jayboy's house, a donkey was tied to a post on the street. When I reached the donkey, it ran across my path I hit the rope. I was thrown in the air. I fell to the ground and seriously injured my body and limbs. I must note also that I was not taken to the hospital for any of my injuries. My father was my doctor. He always treated me by boiling *neem* leaves in water and gave me a bath from head to toe; then he cleaned the wounds with warm water, and applied a salve to the injured parts of the body: hot dye (ground turmeric) mixed with coconut oil and wrapped in a *bond-patai* leaf. He bandaged the salve with strips of cloth to hold it in place.

Chapter 3
My first date

As years went by and I was in my mid-teens, things started to change between Monica and me. Our love for each other was getting stronger and stronger with each passing day, and I was desperately looking forward for that day when I will have the chance to hold her into my arms, look into her eyes and express my feelings to her telling her how much I love her and kiss her.

Within six months my dreams came true when I received a letter from Monica that she would meet me at the backyard of her friend Sharda's house on the evening of my seventeenth birthday. I was counting the days, hours and minutes towards that day.

As the day approached, I cannot forget that evening, when the place started to get dark; and with the help of Sharda's brother Ramesh, I managed to sneak into their backyard adjacent to the fence separating their house and Monica's house. I hid in the backyard waiting for the arrival of Monica; my heart was beating and pounding profusely. I was very nervous not knowing what to expect. The minutes became hours as I waited and wondering whether Monica would manage to sneak out of the house and meet me.

Within a short time, I saw her walking towards me. I then jumped over the fence and waited for her as she approached me, I extended my hand and held hers as she reached me and we started hugging each other. I then, for the first time placed my lips unto hers and kissed her. This was the first time that I ever kissed anyone. It was indeed a wonderful experience. We spent about fifteen minutes in each other arms expressing our love to each other over and over again, passionately kissing each other. We once again expressed our commitment to each other.

From that day we met at least once a month spending some wonderful times together. We also spent some other wonderful times together with the help of Sharda. One day Sharda took Monica to their farm to pick mangoes with Monica parents' approval, not knowing that Jayboy and I were waiting for them at the farm as per the arrangements with Sharda. That day turned out to be another memorable day as Monica and I held hands and walked freely among the trees as we picked fruits and shared them, both of us taking a bite and passing back to each other. Half way in the farm, we stopped under a *sendora* mango tree, loaded with red chested mangoes, hanging almost touching the ground.

We spent a romantic moment under this tree, hugging, kissing and holding each other as the hanging mangoes formed a natural decoration as they swayed from side to side as the wind blew against them and the birds chirped above while feasting on the delicious fruits. This was indeed heaven on earth, a day that I would always cherish forever. We spent about an hour together before filling a bag with mangoes and walked with Jayboy and Sharda to the main street leading from the farm. Jayboy and I said goodbye to Sharda and Monica as we waited until they were out of sight before we headed back home.

Chapter 4
Going to High School

After I graduated from primary school, my ambition was to further my education, so I discussed with my dad that I wanted to further my education by going to high school. My dad at first was not too keen in sending me to high school. He said he could not afford it, because he would have to pay for my school fees and with his salary it was almost impossible. There was also another reason. He wanted me to help him taking care of the cattle, the farm, and the rice cultivation, which supplemented his income. But I was not going to take no for an answer from my dad, because I had all intentions of furthering my education. I felt that his decision was unfair to me. I had no intention to just stay home and take care of our cattle and the farms like most children did after graduating from Primary school.

I wanted to have a better future for myself and my family when I get married, so I compromised with my father, telling him that I would take care of the cattle in the morning and the afternoon, before and after school. On weekends, I would help with the farm work and I would get enough money from selling our farm produce to pay for my school fees. He finally agreed. For the first time, I saw my father almost in tears as he looked at me and said "Son, I am proud of you and I am so sorry that I was selfish not to sacrifice for your future. I want you to make me a proud father someday." He then finally agreed to my plan and I promised him that some day I would make him a proud father.

I started high school, Berbice High School (BHS), when I was fourteen years old. This school was located at New Amsterdam. It was the only High School in the county of

Berbice where I lived and was about twelve miles from my home.

My best friends at BHS were Peter, Mahadeo, and Rohit who lived in my neighborhood. Rohit and I rode our bikes together to and from school each day. We passed by Monica's home so that I could get a glimpse of her. She was always on the look out for me in the morning and the afternoon and would smile at me as I passed by.

During our rides to school, I enjoyed listening to Rohit singing melodious Indian songs and his story telling as we rode our bicycles.

My other friend Mahadeo lived at Albion Front. I visited him frequently. His parents were very nice people, especially his mom, who adored me and offered me delicious homemade food. Many times, she told me stories of the life of early immigrants' women and the many barriers that they had to overcome. She said that she never went to school and so were all other early Indian girls because the Indian customs were so strict that their parents did not want them to associate with boys, they were very protective. She said that she knew my mom and told me many good things about her. I was very curious to learn more about my mom, so I kept asking her many questions. She said that she and my mom grew up in the same neighborhood in Albion Estate Settlement. My mom was very pretty and loving. She was active in *Mandir* (Church) services.

Her marriage to my dad was an arranged marriage as was the custom of Indians. She was only fifteen years old and my dad was eighteen when they got married. She always helped people in need and did much charitable work.

I was surprised to hear that she was a very good singer and had a melodious voice. She sang beautiful *bajans* at the *Mandir* as she prayed and made her offerings to god. She was over joyed when I was born because Indians considered having a son as the first-born child was a blessing and this belief still exists today. My mom and my dad were happily married until her death. Mahadeo's mom tried to offer me that motherly love that I missed from my mother and she encouraged me to visit her regularly.

Mahadeo was in love with one of our classmates, Elena, who lived at Rose Hall, Canje Estate about ten miles from his home. We would often ride our bicycles to Rose Hall on some weekends, just so that he could see his girl friend.

All my friends knew about my love for Monica, and we sometimes talked about our love affairs. They admired my choice and encouraged me to be honest and loyal to her.

Peter, my other best friend, lived at Fyrish Village, the neighboring Village from where I lived. During that time, Peter was in love with one of his neighborhood girls. This relationship continued after we finished school. His girlfriend later became pregnant, which resulted in a bitter dispute between the two families. We pleaded with Peter to marry her because we were positive that this was his child. He did own up to his responsibility and married her.

While I was attending BHS, my dad bought some new clothes for me, which were worn exclusively when I went to school and on special occasions, so there was no shortage of good clothing.

Some of the students who attended my school came from wealthy families, especially a group of eight girls, who were always extravagantly dressed, as if they were going to parties. These girls made fun of other students. One of my friends told me that they made fun of him and other classmate clothes. This group of girls fooled around with wealthy guys, both in school and out of school. Also, at this school, I heard that these rich girls gave me a nickname, "Nerdy Ricky," because I was seriously involved in my studies and was an excellent student and very much loved by the teachers. I could not believe how cruel some people could be.

I must also mention that Monica's elder sister, Chandra, who was about two years older than Monica, was also attending BHS. Some days, I would carry Chandra to school on my bicycle. She knew about the love affair between Monica and me, and she approved this relationship and tried to assist us as much as possible. Some days Chandra helped to arrange secret meetings between Monica and me.

Going to high school was a very challenging period for me, not with the school curriculum but with the payment for my school fees. This school's policy was very strict about paying school fees on time. Often, I was sent home when my payments were late. I remember crying and begging my father for money to pay my school fees. He sometimes sold one of our sheep or goat whenever there was not enough money generated from our farm produce to pay my school fees.

Another major problem I confronted and dealt with was school books. I could not afford to buy books and I waited for my friends to finish doing their homework, and then I would borrow their books. Sometimes, I borrowed the books before my first class.

It was also not easy doing all my chores before and after school. Some of the chores I had to do before going to school in the morning were to milk the cows and take the cows, goats, and sheep to the pasture. On weekends I had to help my dad harvest the cassava, or mangoes, and then fetch them in baskets, which I carried on my head for about a mile, to the main public road where I would board a bus and take the produce to Port Mourant market where I sold them.

In the afternoon after school, I had to cut grass for the cattle and then go to the pasture and bring the cows, goats and sheep home to their pens, where I would feed them grass. Sometimes, a sheep, a goat, or a cow would go missing; I had to search for the missing animal. I did my homework after all my errands were finished. I must also note that I usually got out of bed at 5:00 a.m. and completed my chores so as to be in school by 8:30 a.m.

I also, could not afford to buy lunch, so I took my lunch to school. Later on in the first school year, one of my classmates, Eva became my very close friend. She lived at New Amsterdam and invited me daily to her home for lunch. Her parents were wealthy but very humble; they loved me and encouraged Eva to bring me over. We rode our bicycles to Eva's house and back to school together after lunch.

Most evenings, during the school days, I would sneak out of my house and visit my girlfriend, Monica. At that time, I was in my later teens, and our love affair moved to a different stage. We still corresponded by letters. Everyday, on my way to and from school, apart from riding past Monica's house, so that we could get a glimpse of each other, I also visited her in the evenings, after I had finished all my chores. I would go to my friend Ramesh's home, which was behind Monica's house, separated by a fence as I mentioned previously. Sometimes I'd get a quick good-night kiss from Monica, from over the fence, without anyone noticing. During the weekends, after I had finished all my chores, I managed to spend more time around Monica's house. We would communicate through sign language. At that time Jayboy had married his girl friend, Sharda, and Jayboy moved to his wife's residence; and on some weekends, Monica and I would secretly get together with the help of Sharda.

I should also mention that before Jayboy got married to Sharda, I was involved in finalizing the arrangements for them to marry. I found the courage to talk to our priest, Pundit Ramsaroop, telling him that Jayboy loved Sharda, and he wanted to marry her. The pundit told me that he would talk to Sharda's father. He did, and after hesitating for a while Sharda's father agreed for them to marry because the proposal came from a priest and Sharda's father was not aware that Sharda was in love with Jayboy. He believed that the proposal was for an arranged marriage.

Now that my true friends were married, I was hoping that, with their help, when I was ready to get married, the arrangement would go through as easily as theirs. Unfortunately, it was not so easy.

After I graduated from high school, I hoped to find a job that would enable me to marry my childhood sweetheart. But things took a different turn after Monica's parents found out about our love affair. On one occasion, I was in a confrontation with her brother, because he saw us talking and walking together while she was returning from the store. Her brother reported the matter to her parents. They scolded Monica and warned her not to talk to me. From that day every time I was around the neighborhood, they kept a close watch on both of us. As I mentioned before, they were very protective of her, as was customary with Indian parents and their daughters. At the same time, my father also scolded me for sneaking around and seeing Monica. He knew that Monica's parents would never agree to this alliance because we were too poor for them. Monica's father worked as a supervisor at the sugar factory and her brother worked with the Ministry of Education. My father was trying to avoid my getting hurt but I was too deeply in love to avoid Monica or listening to my father's advice.

One day, I found the courage to approach Monica's mother while she was walking home from the store. I explained to her that Monica and I were in love, which she already knew, and that as soon as I finished high school, I planned to get a job and marry Monica. She seemed to agree to this plan; however, she wanted to lead me into false hopes because she and her husband had devised other plans to separate us. They stopped Monica from talking to me. But nothing could stop us from communicating or seeing each other secretly.

Monica's sister, Chandra continued meeting me at school and during recess period, the two of us would get together and she kept me abreast of the situation that Monica had to endure daily by her parents.

After five years at high school, finally the time arrived when I had to write the General Certificate Examination (GCE) to graduate from high school. I studied very hard for the next few days before I finally wrote my examinations and passed it.

It was a bitter-sweet day as I bade farewell to my classmates. I had lunch for the last time with Eva and thanked her, and her parents for their hospitality. I once again thanked Eva for being a true friend to me.

After graduation I lost contact with Eva until a few years later, I unexpectedly met her at my friend, Mahadeo and his then classmate girlfriend, Elena's wedding function. Eva met me in the hallway and greeted me by hugging me, and then she kissed me affectionately on the lips rather than the cheek. She said to me that she wanted to do that many years ago when we were classmates. I heard from her for the first time that she was in love with me; but she never had the courage to express it to me. She knew that I was in love with Monica and at the time she was unsure of my reactions if she expressed her love for me. She said she is now happily married. I once again thanked her for all that she had done for me. I admired her for standing up to the girls that were bullying and making fun of other students. I told her that she is a true friend and her friendship would always be a part of my memory.

Eva then took me inside the hall and introduced me to her husband. I was surprised that she already told her husband that she had a crush on me during high school days because her husband said to me. "So you are the one that broke my wife's heart. She talked very highly of you and how respectable you were to both her and her parents." I told him that he was a lucky guy to marry such a respected and loving girl, and I knew that she would make him happy.

Chapter 5
My Last Year as a Teenager

I was nineteen years old when I graduated from high school, and as a teenager; I was no longer the shy kid, as I had been when I was younger. I had more free time and found myself doing mischievous teenage stuff. My father did not allow me to go out during the nights but, somehow, I found ways to sneak out, when he was asleep.

I cannot forget one incident on a Saturday night; when I escaped while my father was asleep. I went through the back window and climbed to the roof of a shed that was located at the back of our house. From there, I jumped about eight feet to the ground and sneaked through the back yard. I walked across my neighbor's yard and came out to the street, where my friends were waiting. We then went off to the movies. I returned around midnight, I then dropped off my friend at his home in the neighboring Village; and while heading home, as I turned to go in my block, my bicycle headlight flashed on a body like figure dangling from a tree. I was unsure whether it was a spirit or a real person. I rode as fast as I could, shivering with fright as I rode past the figure. To make matters worse when I arrived home, the window that I left unlocked to re-enter the house was closed. My dad locked it after returning from the outdoor bathroom. He believed that I forgot to close it before going to bed.

As I stood by the front door I was still shivering with fear. I went around the house on a pitch-dark black night trying to find a way to re-enter the house. I was not good in picking locks, so I tried to find out whether any other windows were left unlocked but my luck ran out because all the windows were tightly bolted. I could not go back to my friend's house because I had to pass by the figure that I saw dangling from a tree and also my friend probably already went to bed, and I could not knock on his door because I would awaken his parents. So the only option I had was to spend the rest of the night outdoor. I took three emptied rice bags that were under the small shed. I spread one on the dirt floor and covered from head to toe with the rest as I spent the night under the shed.

During the night I did not close my eyes a blink because I was so afraid that I was shaking with fright, praying for daylight to arrive; and as daylight approached, I hid at the back of the house waiting for my dad to come out of the house, which he did after a short while. He walked to the back yard going to the bathroom which was located at the back of the house. I managed to sneak into the house unnoticed.

Unaware that I was missing during the night, my dad finally came in my room to say goodbye to me before leaving for work. I later found out that the figure I saw was indeed a person from our Village. He hanged himself after a drunken night, quarreling and beating his wife. Afraid that his wife would call the police, he hanged himself. Thank god I did not stop or else I would have dropped dead myself. For the next few nights I stayed at home afraid to go out after dark.

As days went by, I started spending more time around Monica's home at my new friend Suruj's house. He lived two houses from Monica's. I could see her as she walked in the yard or went by the windows looking for me.

One Saturday night, my friend, Suruj and I arranged to have an evening picnic at his home with few other friends including my friend Jayboy. We planned to make cook-up rice with chicken, and Ramesh volunteered to bring the chicken. We were not aware that he took one of their chickens without his parents' knowledge. He told us later that while his parents were asleep, the night was dark, he went into the coop and grabbed one of the hens. He killed it, cooked it, and we had a good party. Jayboy also supplied us with liquor and cigarettes. This was the first time, at age nineteen, that I consumed liquor, and it was also the first time that I smoked a cigarette. After that day, Jayboy and I would occasionally get together, have a few drinks, smoke a few cigarettes, and have an enjoyable time. A year later, I stopped drinking and smoking, with Jayboy, realizing that neither one was good for my health. I must admit that I did not get drunk easily, but I had terrible hang-overs which lasted for several days. I realized, also, that I could never be as good a drinker as my friend Jayboy.

Another incident was a run-in I had involved Monica's father. One evening, I went to meet Monica and while at my friend's backyard, sitting and waiting, I saw Monica's father at his backyard. He went to use the outdoor bathroom, which was located at his backyard. I tried to sneak away but somehow he saw me although it was dark. He became suspicious that Monica was sneaking out of the house to meet me when it's dark. From that day Monica's parents ensured that she was not the last person to go upstairs. They made sure that she was in her room before they went to bed; but that did not stop me from meeting Monica because Chandra (Monica's sister) helped to arrange for me to meet Monica in their house during the night after everyone was asleep. She would leave the downstairs back window unlocked and from her bedroom window she gave me the "Ok" sign when everyone was asleep to enter through the window and sneak into the house.

Chandra and Monica shared the same bedroom so she would leave us in the room and lie on the sofa in the living room pretending to read while Monica and I were in the bedroom. Chandra was at the time a teacher, a job she got after graduation. She normally rode her bicycle to her job and I would meet her on her way to get the latest update on Monica and to make arrangement to meet her at least once a week.

I could not believe that while growing up as a child, as a very shy and quiet boy that I now became so bold and rebellious. I would do anything to meet the one that I was crazy in love with, so that I could hold her in my arms, even if it cost me my life.

One night an unexpected event occurred: when I went to meet Monica in her bedroom. While I was talking to Monica and Chandra was heading out to the living room, her hand accidentally hit a vase which fell on the floor and shattered. The noise awakened her brother, Ron, who came to investigate. Chandra quickly bolted the room door as her brother asked if everything was ok, to which Chandra replied that everything was fine; but Ron came knocking on the door and asked her to open it. I quickly headed to the open window facing the backyard but rather jumping about twelve feet down. I managed to grab onto the gutter of the roof and somehow pulled my body up on top of the house. I lay quietly as Chandra opened the room door for her brother.

Ron had a flashlight for searching the room, and I could see the lights flashing through the window at the backyard. I then crawled to the front half of the "V-shaped" roof as Ron went to the backyard searching with the flashlight. At one point he flashed the light on the house as I hid out of his view. He then went back in the house and went to bed. I could hear him talking to his wife, telling her that he heard a noise on the roof. His wife answered that it was probably the rats and she asked him to go back to sleep. I waited until everything was quiet, assuming that everyone was asleep. I lay quietly on the roof and waited about an hour more, just to make sure that everyone was sound asleep before I crawled slowly to the back of the roof, trying to find a way to get down. I could not jump down because I was about twenty-four feet above the ground. I then remembered seeing a drainage gutter leading from the roof to the ground at the back of the house.

It was a life and death situation as I tried to get to the drainage gutter. At one point my entire body was dangling as I grabbed on tightly to the main gutter praying for it not to come apart. Finally I managed to get my entire body on the drainage gutter and slowly slid down as if I were descending from a coconut tree until I finally reached at the bottom. I then jumped to the ground and ran as quickly as possible, jumped over the fence, and ran until I reached home. That was indeed a close call.

The following day I went to Sharda's backyard by the fence that separated Monica's house, and as I stood there looking where I was the previous night, I could not believe how I got on top that roof. Also the area that I came down had huge wasp (marbuntas) nests. I was surprised that I was not stung.

I must admit that apart from doing all those weird teenage stuff, I was very respectable. I respected my elders. I never drank or smoked in front of adults, or in public; and I did all my chores at home.

After graduation from high school, I was desperately looking for a job. About six months later I finally got a job at the Albion sugar estate local accounting office. Now that I was employed, I thought that Monica's parents would finally agree for us to get married. But I was wrong. They still felt that I was not worthy for their daughter. In-fact they did exactly the same to Monica's sister, Chandra. She was in love with another teacher and wanted to marry him, but her parents also disagreed of this match. So Chandra and her boyfriend eloped and got married without her parents' approval. Her parents could not stop her because she was at the age when she could marry legally without parents' consent.

Chapter 6
Death of my father

As time went by, Monica's parents became more desperate in keeping us a part. They continued scolding her, warning her never to talk to me again; but that did not stop her from talking to me nor did it not stop us from secretly meeting each other. Her parents had no other choice but to seek an arranged marriage for her as per their religious beliefs and customs.

I was already twenty years old and Monica was seventeen years; and upon hearing about Monica's parents' plans, we had no other choice but to elope. With the help of Sharda and Jayboy, I managed to take Monica to our house where my father accepted her willingly. Although he believed in arranged marriage, he knew how much I loved Monica and he also wanted Monica to be his daughter-in-law. I secretly arranged with our Indian priest to perform the marriage ceremony according to Hindu rites in the presence of my dad and my friends Jayboy, Sharda, Ramesh, Mahadeo, Peter, Suruj and Rohit. This marriage is recognized as legitimate, according the Hindu religious belief and Indian customs, but not legal according to the laws of British Guiana. We could not sign the marriage documents because Monica was a few months short of her eighteenth birthday, which is the legal age when she does not need her parents' signature.

Now that we're together, I thought that our problems were finished but little did I know that our problem had just started. Within two weeks Monica's parents brought in the cops. They arrested me and sent back Monica to her parents' home.

I was detained for almost three days without being charged for any crime. I was told by one of the cops that there was no ground for the Sergeant to hold me in detention because both of us were above the legal age of sixteen and were not considered as minors; but according to what I heard, Monica's parents bribed the Sergeant.

Meanwhile when I was released, I found my father in bed sick. He could not bear the stress of witnessing my sufferings. He was a well-respected man in the community and he could not bear to see his character being tarnished. He was so distraught that he suffered a heart attack and a stroke on his left arm and leg. I felt guilty that I was responsible for my dad's condition and promised him that I would spend my life taking care of him.

While I was busy taking care of my father, I did not get to see Monica for a few days. I later received a letter from her telling me that her parents were taking her to her brother's house in the city and they were keeping a very close watch on her and she would not be able to meet me and she once again expressed her love for me. She also mentioned that her parents were forcibly getting her engaged to a boy named Sugrim from USA.

Within two months of receiving Monica's letter, she was sent to the United States. When I received the news from Sharda, my entire life was shattered and crumbling. I was so heartbroken and wished that I could follow her; unfortunately we were very poor and could not afford to go anywhere, and even if I had the money I would not be able to get a visa. To make matters worse my dad's condition took a downturn and he became very seriously ill. He died two weeks later.

Before my dad passed away, he said to me. "Son, I know I do not have long more to live, but I want to tell you a secret of my life before I die". He then handed me a letter and said "I hope someday you will search for my brother who was my best friend. He came with me together from India, but we were separated when he was dispatched to Trinidad. His name is Ramoutar. In this letter I explained everything to him. Please find him someday and give this letter to him. He would be happy to see you".

He went on to say that although Ramoutar is an adopted brother, but he always considered him as his own flesh and blood. He and Ramoutar grew up in the same village as neighbors where Ramoutar became an orphan when he was only five years old. My grand parents (my dad's parents) adopted him; and from then my dad and Ramoutar treated each other as brothers rather than friends. He explained to me that they were about fifteen years old when they left India to go to a foreign land in the hopes of a better life. At that time India was under the British rule and life was very hard. They were almost in starvation because of drought and the strict laws of the British, so when the recruiters came and told them stories about this new land and the opportunity of being rich, they decided to take the risk.

My dad continued "We were living in a small remote village in Bihar, India when the recruiters came and took us on a trailer driven by a tractor. We were then transported by bus, then train to Calcutta where a doctor examined us. We were then placed in holding pens like cattle for a couple of days. Most of the Indians who were in the holding pens came from places such as Bihar, Lucknow in Uttar Pradesh, Karachi, Lahore, Punjab, and Hyderabad, with a minority from Madras. We were held for about a month until the ship arrived. The ship's name was *Rhine*."

My father also told me that before the immigrants left India, they were asked to sign five-year contracts, which none of them could read because it was in English. The contracts did not mention wages, living quarters or health care. It was just a contract that *"bound"* them to work in the sugar-cane fields for five years. There were many regulations on the contract of which the Indians were unaware, such as that they would live in the same quarters vacated by the freed slaves.

Some other clauses in the contract were that they were to perform willingly and diligently their duties as laborers, with the usual time allowed for rest and food; and were they at any time during the period unable to perform their duties because of sickness or other inevitable causes, they agreed to relinquish all claims upon their masters for wages during the period for which they were absent from work.

Another clause in the contract so as not to be a burden to the estate management, one rupee per month would be held from the pay of each individual until there was sufficient sum to provide return passage for each to Calcutta; and should no such contingency take place, the money would be restored at the end of five years.

Based on the contract, they received the following rate of pay, paid per month (varies from estate to estate): superintendents, 16-24 guilders, headmen, 7-10 guilders, laborers (men), 5- 7 guilders, and boys,4- 6 guilders.

Because the immigrants could not read nor write English, their thumbprints were their signatures.

All these regulations were strictly enforced. As a result, the life of the *bound workers* or *bound coolies*, as they were called, was really miserable. They were unable to save any money because of the low wages and also fines that were imposed on them when they missed work or because of trumped-up charges by the estate overseers. There was not enough food and clothing because of rationing by the management. They were even treated like slaves because the same management was so accustomed to controlling the African slaves. There were claims that **slavery in another form was re-introduced.** Some Indians were imprisoned, and many ran away from the plantations only to be caught, charged and even beaten.

My father also said that there were not too many women, as men outnumbered women (40 women to every 100 men). The authorities made little effort to increase the quota of female immigrants, although the shortage was heavily criticized. To make matters worse, some British managers lived with Indian women. This caused some women to be unfaithful to their husbands, resulting in jealousy and murders.

My father then continued telling me how he and Ramoutar got separated. He said "During our journey after we left India, it was a life and death experience with fierce wind and large waves hitting the ship as we clutched to each other shivering and held each other for comfort. When we arrived in Trinidad, some of the Indians were dispatched, including my best friend and brother, Ramoutar, although we pleaded with the recruiters, begging them not to separate us. Our cries were ignored. With tears in our eyes we bade each other farewell. I told him that with God's help some day we will reunite. He then took a pendant that was hanging from his neck and handed it to me. I also did the same and gave him mine, as we promised each other that this pendant will preserve the bond of our friendship forever."

Along with the letter that my dad handed me, he also gave me the pendant, and I promised my dad that I would find Ramoutar some day.

Chapter 7
In search of my Uncle

After my father's death, I was so devastated that I did not know what to do with my life. I lost my girlfriend, the one that I truly loved, and now I lost the one that took care of me and the one who gave me both moral and fatherly support. I was shattered. Monica's friend Sharda and my friend Jayboy were the only ones who cheered me up and gave me some comfort. They became my only friends and they filled the space left with the loss of the friendship that I used to have with Monica All this caring and love eased the pain I felt for the loss of my father and gave me the feeling of family again.

With all the tragic things that went on in my life, especially getting arrested and the things that Monica's parents had done to me, I could not face the public with that respect that I used to have. Although the public did not blame me, I still felt ashamed of being arrested. So to seek comfort and relief from some of my stress, every morning I got up and walked toward the seashore, sitting under a mangrove tree by the wharf, looking at the waves as they flowed back and forth, staring across the horizon as the birds flew over the Atlantic Ocean, thinking about my love who is on the other side of the ocean. I wished I had wings or the magical powers to fly *across the ocean in search for my lost love.*

One day while sitting by the ocean, I saw a ship arriving and docking by the wharf, unloading its cargo. I walked towards the ship as the captain came ashore. He saw me standing by the dock and asked me if I could get him some cigarettes.

I answered, "Yes." The captain then gave me money to purchase the cigarettes and I walked a few blocks to the store where I bought the cigarettes and took them to the captain. He thanked me and then handed me a tip, which I did not accept. Instead, I said to the captain,. "Sir, there is something else you could do for me, I want to go to Trinidad and I would do anything to get there."

The captain said, "It seems that you are a good boy. My next stop is Trinidad. I will take you there providing you help me clean the deck of the ship." I agreed. He then asked me to be at the ship by six o'clock the following morning.

I said "Thank you" to the captain and left for home at my usual time when it started to get dark. I then took my old school bag and packed some of my clothes in it. I also tucked into the bag the letter that my dad gave me along with the pendant. I also had a few letters from Monica, which I cherished. I packed them neatly wrapped into my bag. That night I couldn't sleep; I was thinking about my journey to Trinidad and my only chance to fulfill my father's last wish in finding his brother Ramoutar; and for me, this would be my chance to start a new life.

Early the following morning around 5:00 o'clock while it was still dark, I walked towards the wharf with my bag hanging on my shoulder. I did not tell anyone that I was leaving, not even my best friends Sharda and Jayboy because they were still asleep.

As I approached the ship, I saw the captain examining the ship, making sure that everything was OK for the journey. I said "good morning" to him and he asked me to come aboard. He then brought two cups of coffee, and he called me over to join him for breakfast. As we sat having our breakfast, he asked me about myself, I then started telling him about my dad, about the problems that I encountered with Monica's parents, and the separation from the one that I truly loved. I told him that I could not see myself living any longer in the Village where I was born. He asked me if I knew anyone in Trinidad.

I answered "No, but I am on a journey to search for my dad's brother who was separated from him when they were very young".

The captains asked, "Do you have his address or do you know where he lives."

I replied "No".

The captain felt pity for me and told me that he would try to help me. He said he knew someone that he had a business relationship with in Trinidad and that he would talk to the businessman to get me a job and if possible to get a place to stay. I thanked him. He then introduced me to the rest of the crew as he got ready to set sail.

With tears in my eyes, I stared at the shore of Guiana until there was no more land to be seen. I knew that there was no turning back and that I was leaving my homeland and my past forever. I was also leaving the country, which I considered one of the best places on earth and a tropical paradise with its hidden mineral gems of gold and diamonds and many water falls, including the world's wonder, the magnificent Kaieteur Falls.

Guiana has spectacular beauty, and the abundance and diversification of wildlife and tropical forest where the world's rare species of birds and insects are in abundance, not forgetting the flowers and faunas that grow in abundance with sweet aroma, compounded with the fresh clean air which is indeed one of the world's wonder. It would be hard for me to erase Guiana geological beauty and millions of animals, birds and insects evolution. To me it is truly impossible to say there is only one highlight of this country because there are so many.

British Guiana is the country which I consider my home and the place where I have lived all my life, and now I am not only leaving my beautiful country but also leaving two of my best friends who helped me through out my tragedies and the ones that tried their best to comfort me throughout the disasters of my life. I felt sorry that I did not bid them goodbye before I left because everything happened so fast.

No one saw me leaving Guiana. So after not seeing me for a few days, my two friends went searching for me by the seashore where they knew that I spent my entire day trying to calm my depression and sorrows. When they couldn't find me, the Villagers joined in the search in the many neighborhoods and through the bushes and swamps. They searched the shoreline possibly for my dead body but after a week of searching and not finding me, everyone gave up hope and came to the conclusion that I had committed suicide by drowning and that my body was carried away into the ocean.

When the ship docked in Trinidad and the captain had performed all of his required duties, he took me ashore and introduced me to his acquaintance and businessman named Rohan and asked him if he could give me a job and find a place for me to stay. Rohan promised the Captain that he would indeed help me. In fact he said he needed someone to work in his farm and I could live in his farm house which was vacant.

I thanked the captain and bade farewell to him. I then joined Rohan in his Jeep and we drove off.

During our journey we talked mostly about his business. I found out that he managed his father-in-law's business, which includes cane fields, cattle ranch, rice farms and an Import/Export warehouse.

On our journey to his farmhouse, he stopped at a grocery store where he bought some groceries for me. He then took me to his farm house.

The property was fenced in and at the main gate was a guard who opened the gate for us as we approached. Rohan then introduced me to the guard, telling him that I would be staying at the guest cottage and he should give me access to the property. We then drove past the main building towards the guest cottage and Rohan said, "This is where you will live". We got out of the jeep and walked towards the cottage with the bags of groceries, which he asked me to help him carry. He handed me the keys for the door and said "this is yours along with the groceries". He then followed me into the cottage and showed me around.

He later said, "Make yourself at home and if there is anything else that you need, please do not hesitate to ask me". He offered me a job working, some days in the cane fields, and some days in the rice lands. He said I would receive full salary and free boarding in the cottage. He asked me to start a week later, and I should use the week to get settled in, to know the area and do some sight seeing. He then handed me some money and said that I should use it until I received my first salary. He showed me a bicycle and said I should use it to get around. He then bade me goodbye and left.

I walked around the cottage. It was well furnished. It had a living room, a kitchen and a bedroom. I went in the bedroom, sat on the bed, and took my clothes out of my bag and hung them in the closet. I then went into the kitchen, unpacked the groceries and placed them in the cupboard and the refrigerator. There were pots and pans, I later took a shower and made myself some coffee which I drank as I sat by the stairs looking at the view, and its scenic beauty.

My new surroundings looked very good. On the northern side of the home was the main cottage house. On the southern side was the pasture. At the back of the house were about ten acres of farmland. Different varieties of mango, coconut, guava, banana, and many other fruit trees grew there. They also grew cassava, eddoes, peppers, and other vegetables.

The best view from the house was at the front with vast open lands, which were converted into rice lands. During the off season, the open lands were used as pasture for the cattle. I started enjoying the fresh breeze blowing across the open fields, especially as the evening approached. I then walked to a large tree in the yard and sat on a seat that was built under it, enjoying the cool, fresh breeze as it hit against my face. It was very comfortable and soothing as I stared across the fields.

I could see the beauty of the sunset as the sun went down at the back of the house, creating red streaky clouds across the horizon. The light penetrated through the trees as the sun went down. What a beauty it was. At that moment, I started thinking about my love, Monica. I wish she were here with me enjoying this tropical beauty which would have been such a romantic evening. I sat under the tree until it was dark then walked back to cottage where I spent my first and best night after many previous sleepless nights.

As I woke the following morning, I looked through the windows. It was so beautiful as I enjoyed looking at the rising sun across the open rice fields. Dew fell on the grass and the sunlight reflected on it creating a dazzling reflection as if small pieces of diamonds glittered across the land. This was my daily enjoyable moment looking at the rising sun as it reflected on the open land across the street, especially when the land was covered with water and the sun reflected off it creating such a beautiful reflection.

I saw flocks of birds daily going South in the morning. In the evening, they would come back North. Both times, they flew over the house. I also enjoyed looking across the horizon, especially during the rainy season, when I would see the rainbow with its spectacular colors of violet, indigo, blue, green, yellow, orange and red. All day long, different species of birds flew from tree to tree and flower to flower in our yard. Some birds would whistle beautiful sounds while others gathered nectar from the flowers. Some of the birds that I enjoyed looking at were the Kiskadee, which had beautiful yellow, black and blue colors, with a white circle around its head; the blue saki, which was completely blue in color; the humming bird, which flitted around the flowers daily; and the parrots, which sat on the trees beside the house eating their fruits. During the nights I could hear different sounds of animals, owls and crickets. In the morning, the cocks crowing and birds whistling awakened me. Sweet scents of lilies and jasmine greeted me as soon as I opened the windows. Also, along the sidewalk of the street were beautiful wild flowers that formed a scenic view.

During the morning hours, I took daily strolls through the farm at the back of the house. On my way back, I picked fruits, which I used for snacks during the day. My move to this new area helped me with some of my depression and to be away from the tragic environment. I believe this was the best decision that I made. The area was indeed a tropical paradise. I got adjusted in no time as I started enjoying my new surroundings. It was an idyllic scene that transported my soul in a relaxed state of mind.

The only other building here was the main cottage house. Residential area was about a mile away. Most of the people whom I saw in this area were people going to work or those that were working in the fields or farms, A few tractors and trucks passed by. Some workers rode their bicycles while others came on motorcycles or horse backs and some on foot.

During the first week, I took the opportunity to know the neighborhood, as I rode along the dirt road further down into the fields on the bicycle that was provided to me by Rohan. I could see signs showing "Ram's Rice Cultivation". On the other side of the street was a sign "Ram's Ranch". As I rode a couple miles down the street, I saw vast sugar cane fields with a large sign displaying "Ram's Sugar Cane Fields". I rode through the cane fields about eight miles down the road where I saw large areas of additional rice lands.

As I rode further down the street, I came to a forested area. I laid my bicycle down and decided to walk in the forest. I followed a path a few feet away and stood looking at the monkeys as they jumped from branch to branch. I saw many different beautiful species of birds and not forgetting a green snake that blended itself with the green leaves as it crawled on the tree limb. It was getting late so I decided to start my homeward journey before nightfall, but I promised myself that I would return to the jungle and explore it further.

I reached home as the sun was going down, stopped by the guard at the main gate leading to my cottage. We had a conversation talking about ourselves. He told me that Ram is Rohan's father-in- law and the owner of the properties. He also told me that Ram owns a wholesale distribution warehouse in Trinidad and an Import/Export company in United States of America. He traveled back and forth but spent most of his time in USA while his son-in-law took care of their business in Trinidad. The guard continued that although Ram is a millionaire, he was very ordinary and helped many people. His entire family was very good and loving people. I told the guard that I am very thankful to Rohan for helping me. I then went back in the cottage and made myself some dinner, which I ate before going to bed.

The following day I decided to go the opposite direction where the Village started. I rode my bicycle for about a mile before I reached the first Village. I then continued through the Village until I reached the main public road. I passed by many stores beside the main road. I took a bus to continue my trip to the city, which was about twelve miles away.

As I reached the city I could see many large buildings and huge stores. I was shocked to pass by a building that had a sign. "Ram's Import and Export Incorporated". I then decided to get off the bus walked to the nearby stores, bought myself some fruits and vegetables before I headed for home. I then spent the next couple of days exploring the neighborhood.

Chapter 8
My first job in Trinidad

After spending my first week in Trinidad, Rohan came and took me to the rice fields. He introduced me to the other workers and managers before I started my first day's work. I had experience in rice cultivation while I was living in British Guiana, so it was no surprise what I had to encounter. Ram's company had two different types of rice cultivations. One was done by hand for the low lying areas where it was too waterlogged for machinery to operate and the other was done by machinery.

The first process for the waterlogged area was to plough by hand an area of about half acre, using a hoe or by oxen pulling a wooden plough. Little triangular-shaped dams were formed with the grass and dirt that were removed. This area was used as a nursery for the seedlings.

Then the paddy seedlings were soaked for two days, until they started to form little buds; they were then sown in the ploughed area that was prepared for the nursery, after the water was completely bailed out with the use of buckets or a pump. I remembered in Guiana carrying the heavy seedlings, fetching them on my head to the rice fields. I would go daily to make sure that water did not get in the fields and kill the seedlings. When it rained, I would use bucket to bail the water, whereas in Trinidad I used the pump to get the water out. I rarely used buckets to bail the water, only when the pump was unavailable.

While the seedlings were growing, I made sure that the rest of the land was prepared. In ankle-deep water, workers would use a pair of oxen to plough this area. The area was then cleaned by hand, stacking the grass and mud to the side of the ploughed land. In this process, little dams were formed. We called the dams *"stop-offs."*

After about six weeks, the seedlings were uprooted and tied into bundles, which were then spread throughout the field. The workers transplanted the little rice plants by hand, one root at a time, until the entire field was completed. We took care of the plants, making sure they had the appropriate amounts of water. The plants would drown in too much water and would dry up and die with not enough water.

After four months, the plants started to blossom and the blossoms in a short time turned into paddy. About three weeks before the paddy was ready to be harvested, the water was drained out of field but since this area was swamp most area was still water logged which prevents machinery to operate so the harvest was done by hand.

The manual system of harvesting was very effective in getting a better yield; however, it was also labor-intensive. The paddy straws were cut about two to three feet in length, using a simple hand tool called a *grass-knife* (a circular knife with a handle). The harvested crop was tied into bundles and transported, by head, to the street.

A tractor would then be driven in circles on top the straw bundles, until the paddy fell off the straws. In the meantime, we used pitchforks to turn the straws, shaking them while turning them so that the paddy fell off. After the paddy was separated from the straws, the straws were then removed, and the paddy was bagged and taken to the rice mill.

At the mill the paddy was soaked for three days, placed in barrels, and steamed; the barrels were then carried by wheelbarrows and emptied on assigned concrete decks. The paddy was spread on the concrete decks, about four inches high, and dried for two or three days, while we turned the grains of paddy with our feet every fifteen minutes.

After the paddy was dried they were placed into bags and taken to the mill, where they were processed by removing the shells, and separating them from the grains of rice. The rice was then bagged and ready for export. We also bagged the shells, which was called *bucie*. We took the *bucie* to Ram's cattle farm to feed the chickens and other animals.

This was the complete process for the parboiled brown rice, which is more expensive than the white rice.

As I rode by the rice straws that were stacked at the side of the street, it brought back memories that when I was in British Guiana I had fun playing on the rice straws. We also used the straws then to feed the cattle and to make mattresses and pillows.

The other type of rice cultivation that was done at Ram's rice cultivation was **the mechanical method**, where machinery was mostly used during this process and took place mostly in the interior by the forest where the land was not waterlogged as the area where the hand cultivation was done. This process was done for large-scale cultivation of white rice. The mechanical method of rice cultivation was different from the home-consumption method, and yielded less.

First, the land was ploughed by tractor. The seedlings were then prepared the same way as the small- scale method, by soaking the paddy for two days, until they started to form little buds. They were then taken to the rice field, by tractor, where they were sown by hand and allowed to grow.

One unforgettable incident took place while we were transporting the seedlings on a tractor-trailer, since it was a rainy day, myself and some other workers, sat in a trailer with the seedlings. We had almost reached our destination when the tractor and trailer slipped on the muddy surface and toppled, throwing us to the ground. The paddy bags came tumbling on top of us. But most dangerous of all was when the trailer also came tumbling on top of us. Some of us managed to free ourselves from the paddy bags that pinned us.

We started rescuing the rest. We found one worker who was pinned down by the trailer. The siding of the trailer, pinned one of the worker's foot to the ground. Blood gushed out. Also, under the trailer were two other workers who were pinned. It was a miracle they were not injured. We managed to lift the trailer and pulled the worker's foot out. We wrapped his wound with a piece of cloth. We then managed to push on the side of the tractor and trailer until they were back on their wheels and rescued the two workers. The driver disassembled the tractor from the trailer and drove the injured worker to the hospital, leaving us in the rain, which was still falling heavily. We then carried the seedlings on our heads for the rest of the journey to the rice field, where we waited for the tractor to return for us. It never came because the weather was too bad.

We started walking home, a distance of about twelve miles. It was still raining heavily, and we were soaking wet. We slipped and fell several times on the muddy surface of the street. Meanwhile, our bodies still ached, from the trauma of the falling paddy bags, as we continued our homeward journey. To make matters worse, darkness came upon us when we were only about half way home. It was pitch-dark and we could hardly see the street. Fortunately, we reached home safely around midnight, hungry and tired. I took a shower, had my dinner, and went to bed. We returned to the rice field, the following morning and sowed the seedlings.

As for the rice lands, I went every other week to check on the plants while they were growing. When it was time to spray the plants, some additional workers helped with the spraying and uprooted the weeds, until harvest time.

When the paddy was ripened and ready to be harvested, a combine was used for cutting the rice plants and separating the paddy from the straw. The paddy was filled in bags and unloaded from the combine throughout the field. A tractor was then used to transport the bags to the street, where they were stacked and made ready to be picked up by a truck that would transport them to the rice mill.

I remember one other rainy day. The truck could not get into the interior because the dam was too water-logged and too slippery. We slept in the interior, guarding the harvest for five days, until a truck got in to take the crop to the rice mill.

While waiting for the truck, we feasted on fish and birds that we caught and cooked. During this time, I also took the opportunity to explore the jungle that I visited when I came on the first week in Trinidad.

Once again I enjoyed looking at the various species of birds, and especially enjoyed looking at the different species of monkeys, jumping from limb to limb. As I was sitting on a dried trunk in the jungle, looking at the birds, I saw a large poisonous snake, right beside my foot. It had camouflaged itself under the dried leaves. I slowly and calmly extracted myself away from the snake's company. I also hunted for birds in the interior with a gun that was provided to me by Rohan. Sometimes, I was able to get water from the water-vines that grew in the jungle. This water was clear, but had a fruity taste. During the nights, I had to fight off swarms of mosquitoes. I used empty rice bags to sleep on and under, covering myself from head to toe. As darkness came upon us, I could hear the sound of crickets, owls and most scary of all the animals. I was praying for daylight to arrive.

When the truck did arrive with some other workers, we loaded the paddy bags and transported them to the rice mill. At the mill, the paddy was spread on concrete decks, dried, and milled, using the home-consumption method. The only difference was that this paddy was not soaked or steamed. The soaking-and-steaming process was done only for parboiled brown rice. The white rice was then exported.

Working in the rice fields reminded me of one unforgettable incident I had in the rice fields when I was in British Guiana. One day I went with my neighbor to cut rice for wages, using grass knives. I remember standing, unknowingly, on the back of a huge alligator, which was covered up under the rice straw. Suddenly, I felt the ground moving. I wondered if there was an earthquake; but, after looking down, I realized that the movement was caused by this huge reptile. I calmly walked away. One of the workers killed it with a lance before it could attack anyone.

I must admit that rice is one of the most important meals in all Indian homes then; and up to today, rice still plays a major role in my diet. Rice still remains as one of the staple foods for all Indians in the Diaspora. Even other Indian descendants in other parts of the world, including the United States, Canada, etc, eat rice as a part of their main meal.

Chapter 9
Working in the sugar-cane fields

Now that I had proven my capabilities in rice cultivation Rohan took me to the cane fields. He wanted me to learn all aspects of the cultivation, so I was given the job of cutting canes. At that time I did not realize that Rohan was actually giving me all the necessary training and hands on experience in all departments so that some day I would be assisting him in managing his business.

I started cutting sugar cane, the hardest manual job that was inherited by my ancestors, but I was thankful to be helped by such loving people. I did this for about three months. My foreman was a very nice and helpful man. Some days he would ask me to assist him with doing some of his work, especially the accounting portion. So, instead of cutting cane, I received full payment for those days that I assisted my foreman.

I moved very quickly from one department to another in the sugar-cane department. During the off-season, I planted sugar cane and also worked on the shovel gang digging drains in the cane fields. In a few months I was transferred to an easier job, burning sugar-cane trash, left over after the cane was harvested. About three months later, I moved to the fertilization department. I applied different types of fertilizers on the young sugar-cane plants. Few months later I managed to get a transfer to work in the machinery department, and was responsible for machinery parts.

My big break came about a year later when Rohan visited me and told me that he was impressed by my performance and that he wanted to appoint me as a supervisor. He said that he had found that I was the most qualified candidate for this job, and I had experience in all areas of sugar-cane cultivation: from land preparation, planting, fertilizing, harvesting and inventory control of parts. He also found out that I graduated from high school; and said that if I had told him that I am a high school graduate; he would have offered me a better job when I first came.

That evening Rohan took me home in his jeep. He then drove to the garage at the main building of his farmhouse and handed me the key to a new motorcycle. He said, "This is yours". He also said that on Saturday he would be visiting the farmhouse with his family, and I should join them for barbeque and dinner to celebrate my promotion. I spent the next evening, which was a Friday, riding my new motor cycle to the city doing shopping for new clothes, shoes and sneakers.

When I returned home, I saw a girl at the main farmhouse. She walked over to me and introduced herself. Her name was Rose. She said that she was Sita's (Ram's daughter) friend, and she was there to make preparation for the visit of Rohan's family. I told her, "Please let me know if there is anything I can do to help". She answered that she was spending the evening at the farmhouse and asked if she could join me for dinner. She offered to prepare dinner and I agreed that she should come over to the cottage and we would prepare dinner together. I went in the cottage and started to tidy up the place.

As late afternoon approached, I was neatly dressed waiting for the arrival of Rose. She arrived a short time later with bags that contained ingredients for cooking. As she stood in-front of the door, I could not avoid staring at her. She was a very good looking and pretty girl, but I would not let my emotions take control of me. There is no one prettier than Monica and no one could take her place. I told her to come in and we went directly into the kitchen. She emptied the bags, and I told her to get the rest of the ingredients from the refrigerator and pantry.

As we started preparing dinner together, it brought back memories of those days when I used to help Monica in the kitchen, kissing and hugging her as she prepared the meals.

As Rose was doing most of the cooking, I helped her with the chipping and cutting, as she told me more about Ram, Rohan and his wife whose name I found out was Sita. Rose told me very good things about the entire family. She said that I would be impressed with Sita when I meet her.

Rose then asked me about myself and I told her about my journey to find my dad's brother, and my intentions some day to go to America to find Monica.

When the cooking was finished, Rose laid the tables with our dinner. I rarely drank alcohol but I took out a bottle of champagne from the refrigerator, opened it and poured it in two glasses. I handed one to Rose and took the other. I raised my glass and said "cheers to my new friend". She did the same as I took small sips and she drank hers. During dinner we talked about ourselves. I told her about my life in British Guiana, some of the tragic things that happened to me and about my love for Monica, and some of the happy moments we spent together until we were separated. I also mentioned that I was hoping someday to be reunited with Monica.

After a wonderful evening together, I thanked Rose for a happy evening and how much I enjoyed her company. I then dropped her home and gave her a good night kiss before headed back for a good night's sleep.

The following morning, I got up very early because I promised Rose that I would pick her up and bring her over to the farmhouse so that she could get ready for Rohan and his family visit. After dropping her off at the farmhouse, I went home; then got ready and waited for the arrival of my guests. They arrived a few minutes later, and I walked over to meet them. Rohan introduced me to his wife, Sita. She greeted me with a kiss on the cheek. She is a very pretty girl and had a beautiful smile. She told me that she heard so many good things about me from Rohan. I was also surprised that she also had a little son who was about two years old, whose name is Raj.

I went over to the child picked him up and started playing with him. He is such a cute kid and I adored him. Rose then joined us before we started our barbeque at the deck, which is at the back of the house. We spent the rest of the day talking; I had a lot of fun playing with Raj. Rohan had a few beers and I joined him drinking some wine. Sita stole the day with her charm and beautiful smile. She is such a wonderful person to be around. She told me that she was the only child of Ram, and she also mentioned that she admired me very much, especially my dedication and honesty. She mentioned that Rohan told her about some of the unfortunate things that I experienced before coming to Trinidad, especially losing my childhood love and my dad's death. She wished me the best of luck in finding my dad's brother and she asked if I needed any help, she was there to assist. She also said that I could always turn to them for support and help and she would treat me as her brother. That was the most wonderful day in my life. I enjoyed every moment of it. I also had such a good time playing with Raj. It reminded me of my childhood days when my mom was around to shower all the love and affection to me and I was looking forward to spend some more time with this family. We had a delicious meal together. The barbeque was excellent and so were the rest of meals that were prepared by Rose. We had varieties of different types of fruits for deserts. After such a joyous day, I bade farewell to Rohan and Sita and thanked them for such a good time before I headed back to my cottage.

Chapter 10
My job as a Supervisor

I was very lucky to be promoted as a supervisor. Thanks to Rohan for giving me this opportunity to advance my career and I promised him that I would not let him down.

The following morning Rohan took me to the cane fields, introduced me to the foremen and the rest of the staff, and informed them that I was the new supervisor and was in charge of the sugar cane harvesting department and that they would be reporting directly to me.

During the sugar-cane harvesting season, I worked about eight hours most days, five days a week. My responsibilities were more like a supervisor/accountant. The foreman checked the cane-cutters; the amount of work they completed, the number of punts (pontoons) the cane cutters loaded; and all other miscellaneous payments they received. At the end of the day the foreman gave me a listing of all the payments and then I'd go home and do all the entries each day on wages for over one hundred workers. The workers labored in groups of five to ten and received payments as a group. I had to work out the payment for each individual worker, entering each category of payment separately. At the end, I did a recapitulation of expenses for all employees, by category, and the grand total of all expenses for my department for the day.

I must note that all calculations were done manually-no calculators. Each morning, I dropped off the payroll book to the accounting office where the payroll department processed the entire week payments for each individual employee.

Cane cutting was, and still is, hard manual labor. Each day, I sat under my huge umbrella and looked at the cane-cutters, harvesting the sugar cane under the blazing sun. They bundled the cane and fetched the bundles on their heads to punts, located in the canals, as much as a hundred feet away. Each group of five workers cut and carried over eight to ten tons of sugar-cane daily, with the harsh tropical sun burning down on their backs. They were drenched in their own sweat. On rainy days, the workers were soaked and the wet clay stuck to their bare feet. I sat under my huge umbrella, provided by the estate management, or under a tent, made for me by the workers with sugar cane and sugar cane leaves.

As I looked at these workers, I felt pity for them. This was indeed very strenuous work, and I could imagine what my forefathers went through working in these slave-like conditions. I had a very good relationship with all the workers, and I tried to help them whenever possible. I was loved and respected by all in the area, as well as in the surrounding villages. Not only did the sugar workers look up to me but also their families as well. I was happy to gain the respect that my dad once had.

Cane cutting, also known as cut and load, was the work my parents did as immigrants when they came to British Guiana. This kind of work was passed along to our generation. The manual job of cutting cane by hand still continues today because machinery is unsuitable for cutting the sugar canes in certain areas.

Working as a supervisor gave me the opportunity of meeting many people with different personalities, but I learned very quickly how to get along with everyone.

My salary at this job was very good and now I can afford to do some savings, so as to earn enough money to travel some day to United States of America in search of my childhood sweetheart. Whether she is married or not, I knew deep down in my heart that some day we would once again be together. In the meantime my main task right now is to fulfill my dad's wish in finding his brother, Ramoutar. I found two Ramoutars but those were not the ones that I was looking for because I found out that they were born in Trinidad.

As days went by, Rohan and I started spending more time together and some weekends, he brought his son, Raj, over and we spent some enjoyable moments together. Rohan taught me horse riding and many days we went hunting in the rice land and the jungle riding on horsebacks. Rohan brought an extra gun, which he gave me and he also gave me some shooting lessons. I remember the first time I used the gun was on an alligator that was swimming in one of the trenches in the rice lands. I completely missed the alligator. After then I started practicing shooting cans. I started at close range and increased the distance until I was perfect.

Many days I went hunting by myself in the rice fields, shooting birds such as water hens, carows and spurrings. The birds that I loved to look at were the robins, with their red and brown colors as they flew in the air and dived straight down into the rice fields.

Chapter 11
Monica's Return Trip to British Guiana

As for Monica, unknowing to me, she did not marry Sugrim, the boy of her parents' choice. After almost a year in United States, she returned to British Guiana in search for me with the intention of reuniting and taking me with her back to the United States.

She did not tell anyone that she was going to British Guiana, except the nun, whom she called Mother. So on her arrival in British Guiana, no one was at the airport to receive her. She took a bus from the airport to Georgetown and traveled by train to Rosignal Stelling, then a ferry across the Berbice River, and traveled by taxi to her friend Sharda's home at Kilcoy Settlement.

When she arrived, it was already dark, so the neighbors or her parents did not see her as she entered Sharda's yard. She went up the stairs and knocked on the door and Sharda opened it. Upon seeing Monica, Sharda was shocked and overjoyed to see her standing in front the door. They both immediately hugged as tears of joy poured from their eyes. Sharda immediately helped her with her baggage and took her in the house.

After an emotional reunion, they sat on the sofa as Sharda remarked how happy she was to see Monica after being apart for about a year.

Monica answered: "The main reason for coming to Guiana is to reunite with Ricky who I always considered to be my husband and the only one that I truly love. I now have the opportunity to take him to United States."

Sharda interrupted by asking "What took you almost a year to return and what happened to Sugrim, the boy you were supposed to marry?"

"It's a long story," Monica replied; "I was supposed to go to New York to my uncle's house where my marriage to Sugrim was to take place. My parents would come later for the ceremonies and take care of the dowry and all matters. My parents took me to Guiana airport and booked me on an 8:30 flight to New York. After checking in and kissing my parents goodbye, I had to walk to the gate alone. When I got to the gate, I decided that there was no way I am going to marry Sugrim, since I am already married to Ricky. Fortunately for me the flight was delayed for a day because the plane encountered mechanical problems and when I finally arrived in New York, my uncle, who was supposed to meet me, was nowhere to be seen because I was over a day late. I had arrived in a strange, foreign land where I knew no one and had no place to stay. As I wandered around the airport, I came across a nun and found the courage to talk to her and asked for her help. She asked me, if I had a phone number for any relative or friend. If I did she would contact them and pay the taxi fare to my destination. I replied to her that I have no one in the United States and I had no place to stay. The nun felt pity for me, took me to the airport cafeteria and bought lunch for both of us. During lunch I managed to tell her about my plight and I desperately pleaded for her help. The nun told me that her name is Jessica. 'I am the servant of the Lord and my mission is to help the helpless and those that are in need. I will indeed help you."

As Sharda emotionally stared at Monica and held her hand, Monica continued. "Jessica took me to her home where I spent the night. The following day she took me to the high priest of her church. She asked the priest for his help in getting me a job. The priest then made a few phone calls and managed to get me a job. Jessica also offered me to live at her house where she had a spare bedroom. Jessica was indeed a Godsend. From that day she was always there for me. She treated me as her own child, and I even addressed her by calling her Mother."

As Monica continued telling her story to Sharda, she said; "To answer your questions, first I never got in touch with my uncle or Sugrim and no one knew where I was because I lived in a different borough of New York from them, and I kept a low profile. Concerning your other question, I have a couple of reasons why I took almost a year to return to Guiana. The most important ones are: I was waiting until I reach my eighteenth birthday, which is the legal age when I could marry Ricky without my parents' consent. Also apart from saving up enough money for airlines ticket to return to Guiana, there is another important reason that I will confide to you as my only best friend. I will tell you a secret, which no one else knows except Jessica. The secret is that before I left Guiana. I was three months pregnant with Ricky's child. I never told anyone, not even Ricky because I never saw him again after he was arrested."

Monica continued that six months later upon arriving in the United States, she gave birth to a beautiful daughter and that was the reason why she took so long in returning to British Guiana. She wanted to keep her pregnancy a secret and waited until her child was born before returning.

Sharda asked: "Where is the baby, I am dying to see her". Monica replied that she left her in the care of her friend, Jessica, who became her godmother and the one who helped her throughout the entire ordeal.

Monica paused for a moment and then told Sharda: "I cannot wait any longer. I want to go over to Ricky's house to meet him and give him the good news."

As Monica was getting up to leave, Sharda asked her to sit so that she could give her some details about Ricky. Sharda began by telling Monica that Ricky was not at home.

Monica replied, "Where is he? What time will he return home?"

Sharda then started crying and told Monica: "Ricky is no longer around."

Monica asked, "Where he went?"

Sharda then continued. "After you left British Guiana for United States, and with the death of his father, Ricky was too heart broken. He lost the two people that he loved dearly, and they were no longer there for him. For a couple of days, he spent most of his time by the ocean, sitting by the shore looking at the waves as it went back and forth and the birds feeding on the shore. He was consumed in his own thoughts of sadness. I took meals to his house daily but he hardly ate.

Then one day he never returned. No one saw him again. The Villagers went searching for him without any luck of finding him. Every one came to the conclusion that he committed suicide and his body was taken away by the waves and consumed by the ocean not to be seen again."

Monica then rose to her feet and with raised voice she said "No! No! Ricky is not dead. He is not a coward and would never commit suicide. Furthermore no one saw that he committed suicide and no one found his body because he is alive and I believe he is somehow making his way to the United States in search of me. I will wait for him until I breathe my last breath."

Sharda tried to console Monica as they continued their conversation until the weird hours in the night before they went to bed. It was a restless night for Monica. She was disappointed that she did not meet Ricky; her thoughts were on him for the entire night wondering where he may be, and what he may be going through.

The following morning Monica and Sharda went to my home. It was clean and well taken care of by Sharda. Monica decided that she would spend the rest of her vacation there and brought over her baggage. She did some re-arranging of my personal belongings before heading out to the seashore with Sharda to visit the place where I was last seen.

As they approached the shore, the first thing that caught Monica's eyes was a ship at the loading dock unloading its cargo. That convinced her that I must have boarded one of those ships, and hitch-hiked to the United States by working as a crew hand. She walked towards the ship and inquired from the workers at the dock if anyone saw Ricky boarding a ship at this location. She was told that many ships came in that dock from different countries, and it was almost impossible for anyone except the crew to get on board and travel on those ships.

Monica and Sharda then walked over to the spot where I spent most of my heartbroken days and sat under the tree gazing across the horizon and after spending about two hours they headed home. Monica was now more convinced that I was alive and boarded one of those ships. She spent the night again at my house.

Most of the neighbors saw Monica and came over to express their sympathy of my death to her. Also her parents heard that she was at my house, and they visited her and apologized for their actions towards both of us.

Monica was not ready to forgive them. She told them "For over a year ago, I was dead to you. I suffered so much by the things that you did to me, and most of all the two of you made my life into a living hell. You were the ones that caused the death of Ricky's father and subsequently caused Ricky to go into a deep depression and only God knows where he is now--whether he is alive or dead. Everyone believes that Ricky is dead but I am almost convinced that he is alive and some day I will reunite with him. The only way I would forgive you is if, and when Ricky forgives you." Her parents continued to plead with her for her forgiveness to no avail. They later left with disappointment.

A week after arriving in Guiana and as Monica trip was ending; she spent most of her time with her friend, Sharda. They talked about some of the happy moments they spent while growing up and pledged to continue their friendship.

After a disappointing trip to Guiana, Sharda and Jayboy accompanied Monica to the airport and bade her farewell. But before Monica departed, she said once again that she would be waiting to be reunited with me. She then boarded the plane and departed to United States where her friends Jessica, along with her daughter, were waiting for her at the airport. She was very emotional as she held her daughter in her arms and hugged her. Monica felt some sort of connection with the one that she truly loves through the presence of our daughter.

Chapter 12
The Death of Rohan

Meanwhile as for myself, unaware of Monica's visit to Guiana, I persisted being dedicated to my job and continued helping Rohan and his family. I was very much loved and trusted by everyone, especially by Ram's family. I was promoted to a manager's position and started to handle more responsibilities helping out Rohan as much as I could. I was also given a new Land Rover as part of this promotion.

Rohan continued to be my best friend until the most unforgettable tragic incident occurred. It all started on a rainy day as Rohan was heading home from a meeting, driving through the city. All of a sudden a car approached from the wrong side of the road and was heading directly onto the path of Rohan's vehicle. He swerved barely missing the oncoming car, but lost control in doing so, causing his vehicle to crash into a nearby tree. Some motorist who came to his assistance pulled out Rohan from his damaged vehicle. He was unconscious with blood gushing from a deep wound on his head. He was rushed to the hospital where the doctors tried unsuccessfully to save his life. He was later pronounced dead.

As soon I received news of Rohan's accident, I rushed to his home where I met his wife, Sita horrified, crying loudly, and almost losing consciousness being unable to move. I tried to comfort her before taking her to the hospital where we met the doctor that treated Rohan. He tried to comfort Sita and explained to everyone that Rohan's head injury was so severe, although he tried his best to help him but it was impossible to save his life.

I later took Sita home and then phoned her father, Ram, who was in the United States managing his Import/Export business. I tried my best gradually to break the tragic news to him. He was shocked to hear the sad news and said that he would try to get the next flight to Trinidad, which would be three days later. He asked me to handle all responsibilities until he arrived in Trinidad because Rohan told him about my loyalty, dedication and the most trustworthy employee.

I then made all the necessary arrangements for Rohan's funeral and spent the next three days at Sita's house keeping her company and tried my best to console her. I also helped her taking care of her son Raj. She thanked me for being there as her friend and for all the support that I provided to her.

Three days later Ram arrived in Trinidad. I went with Sita to the airport to bring him home. Upon his arrival, I expressed my condolence to him. He hugged Sita and me and thanked me for taking care of everything after the death of Rohan. This was the first time that I saw Ram and was impressed to witness how humble he was with me.

During our homeward journey, Ram asked me to help him through this tragic period. To which I promised that I would always be there for his family. I told him that I am indebted to them and I would never able to repay all the good deeds that they did for me. I owed my life to them. As I departed home for the night, I promised Ram that I would be there the following morning to help.

That night I could not sleep. My thoughts were on Rohan. He was my best friend and the only one that I turned to for support. I started to miss him already.

The following morning I joined Ram as we went to the morgue and made all the necessary arrangements for Rohan's cremation according to Hindu rites.

During that time the seashore on a dedicated area did all cremation. There was no incinerator, so wood was used instead. According to the Hindu customs, family members and relatives become involved in ceremonies and preparation of the body and procession to the burning. Most Hindus preferred cremation as the method for dealing with the dead.

At the funeral site, in the presence of only male mourners, the closest relative of the deceased takes charge of the final rite. The eldest son or brother normally performed the funeral rites; and since Rohan had no brothers, Ram asked me if I would take part in the ceremony. I willingly accepted and felt that this was the last thing that I could do for Rohan. After the religious ceremony was performed by the Hindu priest, I was asked by him to complete the ceremony of the cremation by lighting the fire on the funeral pyre which I did.

According to the Hindu tradition, the immediate family remains in a state of mourning for ten days after a death. At the end of that period, close family members meet for a ceremonial meal and often give gifts to the poor or to charities. A particular feature of the Hindu ritual is the preparation of rice balls called *pinda* offered to the spirit of the dead person during memorial services. In part these ceremonies are seen as contributing to the merit of the deceased, but they also pacify the soul so that it will not linger in this world as a ghost.

After the cremation of Rohan, his ashes were collected. We took the ashes to the ocean where we eventually immersed them into the water. Everyone then underwent a purifying bath.

As Ram took off his shirt, walked into the water and immersed during the purification bath, something caught my eyes. I saw a pendant similar to the one that my dad gave me hanging on his neck. I asked myself; "Is it possible that Ram's real name is Ramoutar, and is the one whom I am searching for?"

I waited until Ram came out of the water and as he took his towel and started wiping his body, I approached him and asked him if I could take a look at his pendant. He said "Yes". I then held it in the palm of my hand. It was shaped as the left half of the map of India. As I turned it and looked at the back, I was shocked to see my dad's name (Ramessar) engraved on it. I was now positive that the pendant that my dad gave me was the missing right half of the map of India with Ramoutar name engraved on it.

I then looked up staring at Ram and asked him. "Is your real name Ramoutar?"

To which he answered "Yes, but everyone knew me by the name Ram."

Tears of joy started pouring from my eyes because I knew at that moment Ram was actually Ramoutar, my uncle, and the one that I was searching for over a year. He was right there in front of me and yet I kept searching for him. At that moment my thoughts were on my dad. I felt his spirit had guided me after his death. He let me go to Trinidad and guided me to the family of Ramoutar, who rescued and helped me, and now arranged for me to reunite with his adopted brother. What a coincidence and the handy work of god!

As I stared blankly, Ram placed his hand on my shoulder and shook me to take me out of my imagination. He then asked "Are you OK?"

I answered, "Yes, I just remembered my dad. I need to talk to you about him and there is something I want to show you." I then asked him to take me home.

Ram got dressed and drove me home. I was still in shock and did not say much during our journey home. I did not want to tell Ram the secret that he was my uncle until I showed him my dad's pendant and gave him the letter that my dad sent for him. He tried to cheer me up, believing that I was still in shock and depressed over the death of Rohan.

At home, I asked Ram to have a seat while I made two cups of coffee. As we sat sipping our coffee; I asked Ram "Do you know someone by the name Ramessar?"

He replied "Yes, he is my brother. We were separated on our journey from India. I was dispatched to Trinidad and my brother was forced to continue his journey to an unknown land".

I then got up, opened my bag and pulled out the letter and pendant that my dad gave me. I handed the pendant to Ram. He stared at the name, "Ramoutar" engraved at the back. He then placed it together with his to form a perfect match of the map of India and at the back both names, Ramoutar and Ramessar displayed.

Tears started to flow from Ram's eyes as he looked at me and asked. "Where is my brother?"

I told him "Your brother was dispatched to British Guiana, after you were separated from him. He died just over a year ago."

Ram asked if I am related to his brother. I then reached in my bag and told him that Ramessar is my dad. I then handed him a picture of my dad and me.

As he stared at the picture, he started to cry. He then got up, walked over to me and hugged me, telling me that he lost a son-in-law, but found a son. I told him that on my dad's death bed, his thoughts were still on his missing brother, Ramoutar. My dad asked me to someday search for his brother who was dispatched to Trinidad. I promised him that I would make every effort to find his brother.

I believed that the handy work of god guided me to hitch hike my way to Trinidad, and with his help I was able to achieve my dad's last wish in finding his brother.

I then handed Ram the letter that my dad wrote for him before he took his last breath. I could see tears flowing from Ram's eyes as he read it.

Ram said to me "From today you are my son and I promise you that I would be there for you as a father until my death." He went on to say "I am indebted to your dad and his family for adopting me when I was just five years old after both my parents died in a monsoon flood. Your grand-parents treated me equally as they treated their other son and my best friend Ramessar. Your dad and I were childhood friends before the death of my parents and when I moved in with your dad's family, our friendship became stronger as brothers."

I noticed the sadness on Ram's face as he continued; "At that time my grandparents were living a short distance from my parents, but they disowned my parents because my dad married a girl from a different caste, although they strongly objected to this alliance. My grandparents were Brahmin, the highest caste in India and they considered all other caste to be inferior or untouchables. My dad on the other hand believed that all people were born equally and should be treated the same.

At the time my dad was deeply in love with my mom who was his childhood girlfriend and of a lower caste. So when my grandfather told my dad that he was planning an arranged marriage for him with a Brahmin girl, my dad strongly disapproved. My dad told my grandfather that he was in love with another girl of a different caste and wanted to marry her. At that point my grandfather became enraged and said that if my dad refused to marry the girl of his choice that he should leave the house and he would consider him dead from that day. My dad then left, married his girlfriend, and never returned to his parents. His parents then considered him a disgrace to the family and treated him as their worst enemy as of that day."

Ramoutar paused for a moment then continued "Although my grandparents were living in the same street as my parents, they never spoke to each other and when I was born, my grandparents also considered me as an outcaste and never spoke to me. When my parents died, my grandparents did not even attend their funeral. Ramessar's parents and some other villagers performed the funeral rites. Your grandparents took me in as their own son and from that day, your dad and his sister considered me as their own brother".

Ramoutar then continued that their sister was married and after my grandparents' death a few years later, my dad and him were tricked by recruiters who told them untrue stories of opportunity and prosperity that existed in a foreign land called Eldorado, where people walked on gold dust. Both of them were fascinated by these stories and signed up to go to this foreign land and work in the sugar estate.

Ramoutar then went on to describe their entire life-and-death journey as huge waves hitting the ship, swaying it from side to side as water splashed on the immigrants, soaking and making them uncomfortable, many died during this journey.

Ramoutar said that during their journey on the ship, he met his soon to be wife, Radica, and comforted her throughout the journey. After they landed in Trinidad they were separated from his brother, Ramessar. He missed him and his friends very much, and was in a state of depression. He cried for days while other immigrants tried to comfort him. He was later given a job to work as a messenger for the owner of the estate. He was lucky to be the only one selected from his batch of immigrants to be given that type of job. All the rest were dispatched to work in the cane fields.

As Ramoutar sipped his coffee with sadness in his face, he went on to say "During that time, my girlfriend, Radica, whom I met on the ship told me about her dilemma when she was taken to the ship. She said that while in India on one unforgettable day, she went shopping; and while returning home, she was kidnapped and forcibly taken by the recruiters and placed on the ship with other immigrants. She was threatened that if she disclosed to anyone that she was kidnapped, they would kill her. Radica actually came from a rich family and was accustomed to having servants and when she arrived in Trinidad, she became a laborer working in the weeding gang. Although I was in a sad state after being separated from my brother, I tried to comfort her. It was indeed very hard for her to adapt to her new life. She was such a pretty girl that I could not resist falling in love with her. We later got married and had our beautiful daughter Sita."

Ramoutar said he continued to be a loyal worker to the owner of the sugar estate. They loved and trusted him and when indenturship was abolished, the owners of the sugar estate found it very hard to find adequate workers to work in the sugar estate. The estate management gave Ramoutar a large section of sugar-cane fields with the agreement that he would cultivate sugar-cane and sell them to the estate management at a set price.

Ramoutar then became very prosperous and was very much trusted and loved by his workers. He was never short of workers; and as his daughter got older and graduated from college, he decided to expand his business into an Import and Export Company. He once again became prosperous in this endeavor, so much so that he expanded his business by opening a branch in United States which gave him more opportunities to import and export products to and from both Trinidad and United States.

Ramoutar said that he was devastated when after thirty years of marriage, his wife, Radica died after a short illness. His daughter later got married to Rohan and both his daughter and son-in-law helped him to manage the business until the death of Rohan.

One of the most important facts that I received from Ramoutar was that he and my dad had a sister that was married and left behind in India. I was happy to learn that I had an aunt who was still in India. I knew that by now she was probably dead but she may also have children who I was looking forward to meet someday.

Ramoutar then got up and told me that it was getting late and it was time for us to go home. He said my new home will be his house because I am now his son, whom he never had before. I then packed a few personal belongings which I took with me as I headed to my new home with Ramoutar.

Upon our arrival at Ram's house, we met Sita and her son Raj in the living room waiting for Ram's arrival. Sita then asked her father "Dad what took you so long?"

Her dad sat beside her and called me over, held my hand and said to Sita. "You lost your husband, but god fulfilled my wish in finding you a brother." He then went on to tell Sita the entire story about him and my father, Ramessar, their life in India, their journey to an unknown land, his separation from Ramessar and with God's help now, his reunion with me.

Sita then got up, gave me a hug and told me that from the first day she met me, she felt a bond between us as if we were connected in some way, and she was happy to have me as her brother.

I replied to her that from the first day I met her, she was so charming and nice to me that I wished I could have a sister like her, and I also considered her from that day as my sister. Today my wish has been fulfilled and I promised Sita that I would always be there for her as her elder brother. I took an oath in the presence of Ram that I would protect, respect and take care of Sita and her son to the end of my life. I also promised that I would help her with the upbringing of her son Raj, and I would always be there for him as my own son.

After talking for about an hour, we then had a delicious dinner served by the servants. I was then showed my new room where I spent my first night.

The following morning after breakfast, Ram gave me a tour of their house. It was huge with so many rooms that I lost count. This house is fit for a king. He showed me a home office which would be mine to work from home when necessary. The most beautiful room was a room called the "sun room". It was a room that I felt as if I was in an outdoor balcony surrounded by many beautiful flowers. It was enclosed by glass and as I looked outside there was a beautiful garden with many species of plants and trees. Beautiful flower plants lined the walkway and a spectacular waterfall lay beside a sitting area.

Ram then introduced me as his son to the servants, maids, cook, gardener, guards and chauffeur and informed them that

I would be living there, and that they would also take instructions from me. He then took me to the office where he arranged a meeting with all the management staff of his company, including the Import/Export business, sugar cane and rice industries and introduced me to them.

He told them that I would be replacing Rohan and would be in charge of this company. I also promised them that I would treat them no differently than Rohan and I would carry on his legacy. The managements of the sugar cane and rice industries already worked with me when I was a manager and I was loved by everyone. They were happy to learn that I was in-charge of the entire company. Ram then showed me my new office and then gave me a tour of the operations.

We later had lunch in the company cafeteria and then drove to the cane fields and the rice fields before heading back home where we spent the rest of the day with Sita and Raj. Sita was very happy that I would be taking over Rohan's responsibilities because she would not trust anyone else more than me to handle these jobs.

For the next couple of days Ram and I spent most of our time at the office as he gave me the necessary training and tips on how to make the company profitable and successful. I also took a short course in effective writing and presentation skills. I already finished a course in Customer relations while Rohan was alive. Within the next couple of weeks, Ram saw me handling Rohan's responsibilities and was confident that I was capable of managing the business. He then decided that it was time for him to return to United States.

After Ram's departure back to the United States. I took over responsibilities of the business. We had loyal senior management staff including accountant and an attorney who wrote and reviewed all contracts. I attended few important meetings and signed all important documents and all financial expenditures. I received daily updates either through conference calls or meetings.

I started to get more involved in Raj's life, spending more time with him and Sita. I taught Raj to ride a bicycle. He was so excited after I took off the training wheels and the two of us took our bike rides together. Raj was later baptized and I became his godfather. He started calling me dad instead of uncle. I always had breakfast and dinner together with Sita and Raj each day. I must also mention that the first week that I spent at my new residence; Sita insisted that I go shopping with her.

I was not a person that loved doing shopping but she convinced me to go with her. I went with her because I wanted to spend more time with my newly found sister. At the stores, she bought me a new wardrobe including many shirts, pants, shoes, suits, ties. All of different colors, name brands and styles. She then took me to the barber and hairstylist where I was given me a new make-over. I also had a new car.

At the beginning of my new life, it was very hard for me to get accustomed to this luxurious life style. I was not accustomed to servants, maids, guards, chauffeur and gardener. I was not accustomed wearing suit and tie and name brand clothes washed and ironed by servants but the one thing that I loved was driving around in expensive cars.

I cannot forget the day when I spent the first Indian religious day to commemorate the bond between sisters and brothers. This was the day that I took the oath and celebrated the bond between Sita and me. This Indian festival is called *Rakhi* day, which is a day set aside to celebrate the bond between sisters and brothers. In India it is called *Raksha Bandhan* and is popularly known in the Western world as *Rakhi*. It is a popular Hindu festival, which celebrates the bond of affection between brothers and sisters.

The date on which *Rakhi* falls is on the full moon in August. It is the celebration where the sisters tie a special thread known as *Rakhi* around the wrist of their brothers. On this auspicious day brothers make a promise to their sisters to protect them from all harms and troubles and the sisters pray to God to protect their brothers from all evil. The custom and tradition associated with the festival of *Rakhi* reflect the aspects of protection given by brothers to their sisters, and it stands for the forces of righteousness and protection from the forces of evil. On this day people make tasty dishes and sweets at home and exchange gifts. Sita prepared sweets as per the Hindu tradition where sisters for their loving brothers prepare sweets and dishes.

We started the day with an early bath, and then did our prayers, worshiping God. Sita then offered "*aarti*" to me and tied the silken thread of *Rakhi* on my wrist. The day also marked her applying the "*teka*" (vermilion powder) on my forehead. In return I gave Sita various kinds of gifts and presents (including a dress, a watch and a pair of bangles). At the end I turned to Sita facing her and acknowledged the love for her with a promise to stand by her as a brother through all the good and bad times. I then gave her my blessings.

Now that Sita officially became my sister, we started hanging out most of the time. She always consulted me on important matters. Her main responsibilities were to handle all household matters. She sometimes assisted me with some of the office work and did most of the charitable work.

Ram returned to Trinidad a year after Rohan's death for his one-year death religious service, according to the Hindu tradition. After the service we once again gave gifts to poor and charities.

We took our first family vacation a few months later with Ram because he insisted that we deserved a vacation; so he took us on a trip to the Virgin Island where I spent three wonderful days with Sita, Raj and Ram. We had such a great time bonding together as we went sight-seeing touring the island and spent some enjoyable time at the beach. That was the most enjoyable time I had in my entire life. In fact, that was the first vacation that I ever took.

One memorable time I cannot forget was the day when Sita and I took Raj on his first day to school. He did not want to stay; Sita had to stay for a couple of hours with him daily until he got accustomed. After that, I took him in the mornings and picked him up in the afternoons.

Chapter 13
My First Trip to United States

Spending much time with Sita and Raj made our family relationship stronger and stronger daily. I gained a sisterly love that I never had and was enjoying every bit of it. I had a son as my responsibility. I received his affection that I had for the first time, and I also enjoyed every moment with him. I only wished that this child could have been Monica and mine, unaware that I had a daughter living with Monica. Now that I had the opportunity to travel to United States, I was anxiously waiting for the appropriate time to make that trip.

On Raj's first summer vacation, Sita decided to take him to United States of America. She asked me to accompany them so that we can visit Ram and make this trip as a family vacation. I was happy that Sita asked me because I had another reason for going on this vacation. I wanted to search for Monica, and I was hoping to find out whether she was married or not. I still loved her the same as when we were together, and I only wished that she still loved me the same. This vacation would be my opportunity that I waited for so many years to travel to United States. Sita got me my visa which allowed me to travel anytime to USA.

The day that I was waiting anxiously for, finally arrived. As we departed Piarco Airport and the plane took off on our journey to USA, I was thinking that I wished I had this opportunity years ago; but I am satisfied that it is better to be late than never.

The flight was a smooth one because the weather was great. Upon our arrival in USA, as the plane approached JFK airport, it was dark and as I looked at the skyline with its spectacular night view of the city, I felt as if we were landing in a different world as the plane drove on the tarmac and came to a standstill. We departed and Ram was at the airport to receive us. We then drove to his house in Long Island where we would stay during our vacation.

The following morning, I went for a walk, looking at the beautiful scenery and buildings. A few blocks away I came upon the ocean and a beautiful beach where early bathers were already swimming. I went by the shore, sat on a huge rock looking across the Atlantic Ocean. I knew that on the other side of the Ocean far away lies Trinidad and Guiana. My thoughts went back to the days when I used to sit on the other side of the ocean in Guiana, gazing as the waves went back and forth thinking about Monica who was on the other side in United States of America. I am fortunate that now I had the opportunity to sit on the same side where Monica now lived. My only problem was finding her in this large city. I don't know where she lived. I didn't have a clue where to start looking for her.

After spending about an hour by the ocean, I went back to Ram's house and started my first task of finding Monica. I started searching through the phone directories. I came across about fifty names of Monica's and I called those numbers but was unsuccessful in finding her. Later during that day, I went sight seeing with Sita and Raj. We drove through Long Island heading to Queens. I kept a lookout for any sign of Monica, especially by the bus and train stops, also by the malls because I knew that she loved shopping, but there was no sign of her.

The second day of our vacation, I decided to accompany Ram to the office in Manhattan. Sita also decided to go with us accompanied by Raj. Upon arriving at the office, Sita decided that she would take Raj to do some shopping and sight seeing while Ram and I did some work in the office.

Sita took Raj to a toy store because she wanted to get him some new toys to take back to Trinidad. While Sita and Raj were browsing through the store, Raj went to an isle where he was looking at many beautiful toys. Beside him was a pretty little girl who was also checking out the toys. They started a conversation and Raj found out that her name was Sharmila and they talked about the different toys. This girl was very much interested in a play house and she said to Raj "Isn't this beautiful?"

Before Raj could answer, Sharmila's mom came over and started a conversation with Raj and Sharmila. Sita also went over and said "Raj, so you found a new friend. Who is this pretty little girl? She is so adorable."

Sharmila's mom then introduced herself to Sita. "Hi, I am Mona and this is my daughter Sharmila." Sita then introduced herself and Raj to Mona.

Both parents started to chat while the two kids were having fun with the toys. They spent about an hour shopping together. Mona said that she was shopping for her daughter's birthday gifts. She also invited Raj and asked Sita to bring him to Sharmila's birthday celebration which would be held on the following Saturday. Mona then gave Sita an invitation card with the necessary information before saying goodbye. "See you on Saturday." Sita hugged Sharmila and headed to her car. She then drove back to the office where we met before heading home. During our homeward journey, Sita told me all about her new friend and her daughter.

For the next few days we went sightseeing and visited many historical landmarks. We visited the Empire State Building where we went to the top floor balcony getting a good view of the city's skyline. One day we went to the Statue of Liberty. It was a spectacular view as we walked in the Statue to the balcony looking across the Hudson River getting a good view of New Jersey, Brooklyn and Staten Island. We also toured Ellis Island, reading some historical signs that displayed names of the early immigrants to United States and also admiring the architectural beauty of the statue and the Island.

Another day we took a trip to Manhattan during the night. This was one of the memorable moments as we crossed the Brooklyn Bridge looking at the beautiful lights that stretched across the bridge and it reflected with glowing colors on the river below. Also from a distance we could see the beauty of Manhattan as the bright lights glittered from a distance. We passed by Penn Station and Time Square where the subways and trains interconnected to the entire United States. At Time Square lies the beauty of the city with its flashing billboards and its night life. This is indeed the city that never sleeps, as we saw people walking the busy city street even during the late hours of the night. As we headed back home my thoughts were on the beauty of this city that I had previously only seen in movies, never expecting that someday I would be looking directly at these sceneries.

As the day of Sharmila's birthday approached, Sita asked me to take her and Raj to Manhattan to buy her a birthday gift. We went to the same toy store where they met. As we entered the store, I asked Raj what he wanted to buy for Sharmila. He took me to the aisle where he and Sharmila met and showed me the play house and said that Sharmila loved this toy. Sita picked the toy and placed it in her shopping cart. She said to me that she also saw Sharmila asking her mom for it, but she probably did not buy it because of the price tag. I then picked up three beautiful dolls and said to Sita, "These go perfectly with the play house." I placed them in the shopping cart and told Sita. "These dolls are my gift to Raj's friend, Sharmila."

On the day of Sharmila's birthday, Sita took Raj to the hall where there were many other kids, mostly from Sharmila's school and a few of her neighborhood friends. There were also a few parents who accompanied their kids. Mona greeted Sita and Raj, and then introduced them to some of the other parents. She also introduced Jessica, Sharmila's godmother, and her best friend. When Sharmila saw Sita and Raj, she ran towards them and gave them a hug.

Raj then gave her the gift that he bought for her and also the dolls, telling her that the playhouse was from his mom and him, and the dolls were from his dad. Sharmila was so overjoyed with the presents that tears started to flow from her eyes with excitement, as she kept saying "thank you." She then held Raj by the hand and took him to her other friends where they all played together as Sita and Mona spent time discussing some of the events that were planned for the day.

When the time came for cutting of the cake, Sharmila asked her mom if Raj could cut the cake with her, to which her mom gave approval. As Sharmila cut the cake, Raj fed a piece to Sharmila and in turn Sharmila placed a piece in Raj's mouth and they hugged each other. Sita as well as Mona became very emotional as they looked at each other. Raj and Sharmila later played with the rest of the kids until the party came to an end. Sita and Raj said goodbye to Mona and Sharmila, and they promised to see them again before departing to Trinidad.

I spent the next couple of days searching for Monica, traveling through the length and breadth of the five boroughs of the City of New York, Queens, Bronx, Manhattan, Staten Island and Brooklyn. I visited many stores looking for her, knowing that Monica loved shopping. I traveled in the morning and evening when most people traveled to and from work hoping to find her at the bus or train terminals but I was unsuccessful in finding her.

As our vacation was coming to an end, we decided to spend the last day at Jones Beach on Long Island. Sita invited Mona and Sharmila to join us; unfortunately Mona had to work and could not join us but she sent Sharmila with her best friend Jessica to meet us at the beach and spend the last day with us before our departure. We arrived at the beach around ten o'clock in the morning. I left Sita by the entrance to wait for Sharmila while I staked out an area where we would spend the day.

I waited for about thirty minutes gazing at the ocean, day dreaming. Sita tapped me on my shoulder, and as I turned to look at her, I could not believe my eyes as I saw this pretty little girl standing beside Raj. Sita then introduced Jessica and Sharmila to me but before I could say a word as I got up Sharmila hugged me and said "Thank you for the toys." She reminded me of Monica as I could vaguely remember her as a child. The first question I asked Sharmila was "What is your mother's name?"

She replied, "My mommy's name is Mona." Jessica apologized for the absence of Mona because she had to work. We spent a wonderful and memorable day together. It was indeed enjoyable spending time with the kids, as I helped them build sand castle, playing soft ball and eating our snacks with them. I was impressed by the various and exciting activities available here. I took a stroll on the shoreline with Raj and Sharmila, exploring the beautiful shoreline, holding their hands as they playfully waited for the waves to come on shore hitting their feet as they held tightly to my hand. They picked different types of shells and held hands as they walked along the shoreline. As I looked at the two of them, I started having flashbacks of the happy childhood days Monica and I had together. I only wished she was here with me, not knowing that some external forces had brought these two children together.

After an enjoyable time, we headed back to where Sita and Jessica were waiting for us.

I found Jessica to be very friendly and a caring person. She loved Sharmila and took good care of her, and I admired her talented conversation and her soft spoken voice.

Before heading back home, I took them to a nearby restaurant where we had an appetizing meal before we said goodbye to Sharmila and Jessica. As we hugged Sharmila and bade her farewell, I could see the sadness in her face when we drove off.

The following day with mixed emotions, we said goodbye to Ram as we departed for Trinidad. I was disappointed that I did not accomplish my mission of finding Monica but was happy in discovering the beauty of America and spending some wonderful time with Sita, Raj and not forgetting the day that I spent with Sharmila, and the memories she brought back of Monica as a little girl.

After my first trip to United States. I made many more subsequent trips and continued searching for Monica but was unsuccessful in finding her. I never gave up hope that some day I will meet her again.

Chapter 14
Raj departed to College

As years went by our business continued to flourish. I continued being dedicated to my family responsibilities to Sita and Raj and we continued spending enjoyable times together. Raj continued calling me dad, as he started doing the first day when he was told that I was his godfather. He thought at that tender age that I was really his father and he grew up respecting and loving me as his biological father. He always listened and followed my advice. I always treated him as my own son and I was always there when he needed that fatherly love. I enjoyed every moment as I took care of him and seeing him grow up to be a young teenage boy.

Raj started high school when he was fourteen years old. He was involved in sport activities, especially cricket and soccer. I always found time to be at his games when there were competitions with other teams. He had a few schoolmate friends that he also spent time with.

During Raj's teenage life, he started spending more time with his friends, and I started spending more time with Rose. She was a very good friend to me. I knew that she felt more than friendship toward me. I told her many times that I cannot marry anyone else because I was already married to Monica, not legally but we took the vows during a religious marriage ceremony in the presence of close friends and my father. Rose cared a lot for me and was always there for me when I needed a hug.

Many times as we held hands walking on the beach, I felt as if I was holding Monica's hand and I would kiss her, imagining that I was kissing Monica.

As years went by, I went to the United States at least twice yearly in search of Monica but I was unsuccessful. My hopes of finding her started to fade and I must admit that I started having an affair with Rose after fifteen years of being apart from Monica. Although I still loved Monica a lot, I was beginning to have doubts of us ever being together. I started to believe that Monica was probably happily married with children. Even if that was true, and even if she indeed loved her new husband, I would be happy for her if she was happy, but I am longing to see her just once more to make sure that she was happy.

I continued spending much more time with Rose who was also Sita's best friend. The three of us would go out together. I also made sure that I balanced my time with Rose so that I can also spend some quality time with Sita and Raj.

After Raj graduated from high school, he decided to go to New York University in United States. It was indeed an emotional day as Sita and I took Raj to the airport and we said goodbye to him as he departed for College. He decided that he would stay in the college dorm. He grew up all his life in luxury with servants, maid, and cooks. He felt by staying in a dorm, he would get the experience of being by himself and learn to do the basic everyday things for himself. While in college, he wanted to live as an ordinary boy so he kept his family as being wealthy a secret so that he would also blend in with other ordinary students.

During his College days, he called Sita and me daily. We told him how much we missed him. He also said he missed us very much. He told us that he spent most of his weekends with his grandfather, Ram, and that he would spend all his summer holidays and Christmas with us in Trinidad. We were very happy when he came home for his first holiday. We had such an enjoyable time together.

One unforgettable day during Raj's second year in College, I received a phone call from him; he sounded very happy and excited as he said to me, "Dad, I met a very pretty girl and I think I am in love."

My answer to him was "I am so happy for you. Who is the lucky girl?"

Before telling me the girl's name, Raj started to tell me how they met. He said that while he was in the cafeteria having lunch one day, this beautiful girl came in and asked if she could sit and have lunch on his table. Raj continued, "As she sat opposite me, both of us kept staring at each other as if we had met before. I then said to her. You resemble someone that I met before. Have we met previously?"

The girl answered "I believe so. What is your name?"

Raj answered "My name is Raj."

She smiled and said "My name is Sharmila. I believe that we met about ten years ago on my seventh birthday. I could never forget you because I still kept the dollhouse birthday gift that you gave me and above it on the wall of my bedroom is a picture of the two of us cutting my seventh birthday cake. I looked at it everyday day for the past ten years remembering you for all those years, wondering if I would ever meet you again. You look even more handsome than I imagined you to be." Raj and Sharmila then hugged each other and from that day they were inseparable.

I told Raj that there could never be a better choice for him than Sharmila, and I wholeheartedly accepted his choice and I was looking forward for him to bring her on his next summer vacation. He promised that he would do so. He then gave the good news to Sita. I could see the happiness on Sita's face as she looked at me and said that from the first day she met Sharmila, she wished when Raj grew up he would fall in love and marry a girl like Sharmila. She was a little beautiful angel when she was a child, and Sita said she could imagine how beautiful she was as a teenager.

Raj and Sharmila continued dating, spending most of their free time together. As their summer vacation approached, Raj asked Sharmila that he wanted to meet her mom, to which Sharmila replied that her mom was very strict. She was not aware of their relationship and she was afraid of her reaction. Sharmila promised Raj that she would talk to her mom.

Sharmila waited until Saturday when her mom was not working. As they were having dinner, she found the courage to bring up the topic. She asked, "Mom were you ever in love?"

Sharmila's mom looked at her and paused for a moment, wondering what prompted her to ask such a question after so many years. Her mom then replied, "Yes. I was deeply in love with my childhood boyfriend who happens to be your dad. He was the only one that I ever loved and still do".

Sharmila then said to her mom that she wanted her to meet a good friend of hers and asked if it would be ok for her to bring him next Saturday. Her mom looked at her shocked to hear that Sharmila had a boyfriend.

She then asked "Who is this boy?"

Sharmila replied, "Mom, you already met him and his mom when he was a kid. His name is Raj and he is attending the same college with me. He is the boy in the picture on my bedroom wall."

Sharmila's mom, Mona, was relieved to hear that Raj was Sharmila's boyfriend. She remembered him as the cute little boy at Sharmila's birthday. She gave the ok and Sharmila ran to the phone and called Raj to give him the good news, and they made arrangements to meet Mona.

The day before Raj went to meet Sharmila's mother, I received a phone call from him. He was very excited but nervous as he asked for my advice. I told him to just be himself and tell Sharmila's mom the truth about his feelings toward Sharmila. I wished him best of luck and I was very happy that he would not go through the same problems that I encountered when I fell in love.

On the day of his meeting with Sharmila's mom, Raj bought a bunch of red roses, which he took for Sharmila. As he arrived at her apartment building, he sat in his car waiting for a while, trying to calm his nervousness. He was very happy when he saw Sharmila looked through the third floor window and waved at him. She then went outside, held Raj's hand as she escorted him in her apartment. He then handed her the bunch of roses. He was introduced to Sharmila's mom who said to Raj that she was very happy that her daughter met him because Sharmila grew up talking about him and his family for many years. She loved Raj's family and was hoping that some day she once again would meet him and his family. Her wish is now fulfilled.

As they sat for dinner, Raj was surprised to see all the many delicious Indian dishes that were prepared. He enjoyed the home- made food and complimented Mona on her cooking. After dinner Sharmila took Raj to her room and showed him the playhouse that she kept for ten years. Raj was also surprised to see the dolls that his dad bought were in the playhouse. He smiled as he saw the picture of him and Sharmila as children hanging on the wall. Before saying goodbye, Raj asked Mona if she would allow Sharmila to go with him to Trinidad to meet his family and spend summer vacation with them. Mona answered that if it was ok with his family, she would not have a problem sending her. Raj replied to Mona that his parents already agreed and that they were the ones that requested for him to take Sharmila to Trinidad for her summer vacation.

After Raj said goodnight and departed, Sharmila did the cleaning and washed the dishes as her mom sat on the sofa thinking about the happy days she spent together with Sharmila's dad, the one she truly loved before their separation. She wished that her parents could have done the same as she did for her daughter. She had made a promise to Jessica when Sharmila was born that when her daughter became an adult and who ever Sharmila wanted to marry, she would never object to her choice and would support her all the way. She proved it today by accepting her daughter's choice.

Chapter 15
Sharmila's vacation in Trinidad

After Raj's first meeting with Sharmila's mom, he continued visiting Sharmila's apartment nearly every Saturday as her mom prepared home made dishes for them. Raj was surprised to find Mona very humble, loving and care giving. After spending time with Sharmila, he would later visit his grandfather on Long Island where he spent the weekend.

The day finally approached when Raj and Sharmila said goodbye to Mona as they departed for their vacation. That was the first time Mona and Sharmila would be apart for a long period. In-fact that was the first time Sharmila was leaving United States. Raj promised her mom that he would take good care of her and he would make sure that she phoned her every day. Mona had previously met Raj's mom (Sita), and she felt comfortable that Sharmila would be in good hands in Trinidad.

Sita and I went to the airport to receive Raj and Sharmila. We arrived early, so we went browsing in the terminal where we bought some snacks, eating them as we looked at small planes landing and taking off. The airport was not busy because not too many overseas planes landed at this airport. As we continued staring at the runaway, we finally saw the arrival of the North American airline, which originated from New York and the plane that Raj and Sharmila came on to Trinidad.

We quickly went to the arrival section where we waited as the passengers went through customs. I finally saw Raj and as I saw Sharmila, I nearly fainted; she was an identical picture of Monica. She looked exactly like her and was about the same age as the last day that I saw Monica. I got goose bumps and tears came out of my eyes as they walked towards us. I felt light-headed and my feet became weak and I was barely able to stand. Raj came over and hugged me. I kept staring at Sharmila. I could not believe my eyes, as I kept rubbing them making sure that I was seeing clearly and it was not just my imagination. Sharmila then gave me a hug, as I welcomed her to Trinidad. I still kept staring at Raj and Sharmila as we walked towards our car. Raj asked me if I was feeling ok and I told him that I felt a little weak. He said that he would drive home, so I asked Sharmila to sit at the front with Raj while Sita and I sat at the back seats. As I kept looking at Sharmila, I could see the same face, the same eyes, the same hair; she walked and talked the same as Monica. This could not be a coincidence. I started to wonder if Sharmila could be the daughter of Monica and I could not stop myself from asking her. "Sharmila, what is your mother's name?"

She replied that her mother's name was Mona. I then asked her "Who is your father?"

She replied "I never saw my father; my mom told me that he died before I was born. Would it be ok if I call you dad as Raj did? I respected you as my father from the first day I met you"

I replied to her, "It would be an honor and since you will marry Raj some day. I would be more than happy for you to start calling me dad now." Raj also gave his appreciation as he told us about his wonderful experience at Sharmila's home and kept praising her mom. He told us about the playhouse, the dolls in it and the picture in Sharmila's bedroom. Sharmila once again thanked Sita and me for the wonderful gifts that we gave her. She said that she cherished them as her memory for the past ten years.

Sita then replied to her. "Your memory and your destiny have led you once again to us. It is God's handy work and I know you will forever be a part of our family and we wholeheartedly accept you."

As we arrived to the entrance of our home, the guard opened the gate and saluted us and the view of our large house was a short distance away.

Sharmila looked at us and asked, "Where are we going? Whose house is that?" pointing to the house.

Raj looked at her and smiled "It is our house and this is where we live."

Sharmila then said, "Raj you never told me that you were wealthy!" To which Raj replied with a smile "You never asked."

As we reached the house, the butler came and took the suitcases to the house. Sharmila was in for more surprises as we entered the house and she saw the servants greeting us. Raj then gave her a tour of the house, showed her the guest rooms, and asked her which room she wanted. She asked Raj which was his bedroom. Raj then took her in and gave her a tour of his bedroom. She said she wanted the room opposite his. Raj then told the butler to bring the suitcases to their respective rooms.

After touring the house, Raj took Sharmila for a tour on the lawns of the compound. I saw them holding hands, walking through the beautiful flower garden; my thoughts were going wild, imagining those romantic days that Monica and I spent together, especially the day that we walked hand in hand in the farm. I started once again to think of Monica very much.

During dinner, as we were served by servants, Raj noticed that Sharmila was uncomfortable. She was not accustomed to be served by servants, so Raj held her hand and said to her that she was welcome to take her own meals. Raj then passed the dishes to her as she took a little of everything. During meals Raj tried to make Sharmila more at home, so he brought up many conversations relating to the wonderful times he spent with her and her mother.

The following day, we took Sharmila for a tour at the fields. She never saw sugar-cane cultivation, so she was impressed to see first hand as workers harvested sugarcanes. She even took a piece of sugar cane and chewed on it. She also took a stroll with Raj in the young sugar cane fields, which were only about knee- high in height.

We then visited the rice lands. She also never saw rice cultivation. Raj picked a bunch of paddies that were still hanging on the stems and opened the shells to expose the rice inside. He then explained to Sharmila the entire process of rice.

We later visited the cattle farm where Raj took her to the horse stable. He told her that the following day he would teach her horse- riding. We then dropped by the farmhouse where Raj took her for a tour. They also went in the farms as I waited for them in the farmhouse. When they returned, I could see the happiness in Sharmila's face. She picked some fruits and she was eating a mango as they joined me for our homeward trip. She told us that she spent one of the best days of her life and she thanked us for making this a memorable one.

The following day Raj took Sharmila for training on horse riding. He led the horse holding the reins as Sharmila tried to steady herself on the horse's back. Raj then joined her sitting behind her on the horseback, holding her as they both held the reins and they rode away.

As Sharmila became comfortable riding, Raj left her to ride by herself as he rode on another horse beside her. They spent most of the day going through the fields gazing at the birds, animals and the beautiful wild flowers that lined the sides of the street. After another wonderful day, they returned home where Sharmila told us about their fun-filled day.

For the next few days, we spent most of the days together as a family vacation. We went sightseeing touring many areas in different parts of Trinidad and Tobago, including the city, markets and Government buildings. We visited most of the beaches on different days.

One day at the beach as I relaxed by the shore enjoying the waves as the cool breeze blew against my wet body, I saw Raj and Sharmila building sand castles and they carved each other's names on the sands as a huge wave washed them away. I looked at them as they playfully ran against the waves and grabbed each other as the waves hit them. They were having such a good time.

We spent another beautiful day at the farmhouse barbequing. Rose also joined us. We had a family fun day as I enjoyed spending some more wonderful moments with Raj and Sharmila. I once again looked at them having fun together as they loved playing around with each other; I started to get flashback on those days when Raj was a young boy running around as we played together. Most of the day, I kept bringing up Monica over and over again to Sita as I described the resemblance of Sharmila and Monica. I couldn't help my reactions as I saw the wonderful relationship between Raj and Sharmila and my thoughts were on the happy days I spent with Monica.

I could see uneasiness in Rose and I believed that she was uncomfortable because of my actions.

After Raj and Sharmila spent a month with us, they returned to United States. Before leaving, Sharmila thanked us over and over again for a once in a life-time vacation. She said she would always cherish those wonderful moments that we spent together, and she considered us as her own family. Every time she talked to me she called me dad. I felt a close attachment to her as if she was my own child.

After spending such an enjoyable vacation with Raj and Sharmila, my thoughts for Monica once again caused sleepless nights, so I told Sita and Rose that I was planning to be more aggressive in my search for Monica, and I decided to visit Guiana in search for any information on her whereabouts. I wanted to find out whether she ever returned to Guiana or if anyone had her address in United States. I was planning to get as much information as possible while in

Guiana, mostly from her friend Sharda. And upon my return from Guiana, I would travel to United States and if possible seek the help of Raj, Jessica, Sharmila and her mother but my main mission on this visit would be to find her.

Chapter 16
My trip to British Guiana

A week after Raj and Sharmila returned to United States, I could not wait to go to British Guiana. So the following Monday, I took the next flight to Guiana which was in the afternoon. It was a short flight about forty minutes when I arrived at Atkinson Airport in Guiana.

I took a taxi from the airport to Georgetown car park where I hired a taxi that operated from Berbice to Georgetown.

It was around four in the afternoon as we departed Georgetown on our journey to the county of Berbice. The last ferry that operated across the Berbice River was 8:00 PM, so we had enough time. It was already dark as we arrived at the Rosignal Stelling waiting for the arrival of the ferry Torani. I could see the ferry across the other side of the Berbice River on its journey towards us.

After the arriving passengers departed from the ferry, the vehicles were then unloaded. We then boarded the ferry sitting in the taxi as it parked on the lower deck of the ferry. I then went to the upper deck, sat on a bench looking across the river as the ferry departed. This was the first time that I ever used the ferry, although I was living only about twelve miles away. As we approached the other side of the River, I went back to the taxi as the ferry docked at the New Amsterdam Stelling and we departed for our twelve miles journey to Kilcoy Settlement. The place was dark as we came across herds of cows at the side of the road. In one instance the chauffeur had to slam on his brakes as the cows were crossing the road. Also the ride was a bumpy one as we landed on many potholes. The chauffeur was from a neighboring Village of Albion Estate and during our conversation I managed to convince him to be available to take me wherever I wanted to go for the next two days.

After about fifteen minutes from New Amsterdam, we finally arrived at Albion Road; then traveled a mile inland. We passed by the sugar factory and some of the cottages that were still there before arriving at my destination at Kilcoy Settlement.

I was very nervous as the taxi stopped in front of Sharda's residence. It was my first trip back to Guiana after about seventeen years. As I looked around in the dark, there was still no electricity. I could see the lights of lamps in the houses. The houses looked old and some needed major repairs.

I told the chauffeur to wait outside as I opened the unlocked gates, walked up the stairs of Sharda's house, and stood in-front the doors wondering whether she still lived at that house. I was unsure also of her reaction when I meet her.

I then knocked on the door as someone answered, "Who is it?"

I replied," I am a family friend."

A young boy about sixteen years old opened the door and asked. "How can I help you?" I then asked him if Sharda lived there. He replied, "Yes" as he called "Mom, someone is here to see you."

As Sharda came walking towards the door, I was looking at the street to make sure that the taxi was still there and as I turned facing Sharda standing at the door, she stared at me for a moment and then she screamed, "Ghost! Ghost!" as she ran back in the house.

I was still standing at the door and I called out "Sharda, I am Ricky."

She replied, "Ricky is dead, you are Ricky's spirit."

The door was still open so I walked in as Sharda was still shivering. Her son came to me and I told him that I was a friend of Sharda and Jayboy. I was away for about eighteen years and I am not too sure why his mom felt that I was dead.

His son said to me that his mom told him stories about me and Monica and that I committed suicide. He also said that they took care of my house since I went missing.

Sharda's son went over to his mom, held her hand and brought her to me, as she still looked afraid. She touched my hand making sure that I was there in the flesh. She then hugged me and started to cry, as she said, "Where have you been for so many years? Everyone believed that you were dead."

I replied, "It is a long story, but I am not too sure why everyone came to the conclusion that I died."

Sharda then told me to have a seat as she went in the kitchen, made some tea and gave me some cakes with the tea. She then sat beside me, held my hand and started giving me details from the time I went missing. "The last time anyone saw you was by the sea shore. No one saw you returning home. We went searching for you. The neighbors also joined us. We searched for days, looking by the shorelines and the neighborhood but we could not find any trace of you, and since the last place you were seen was by the sea shore, we came to the conclusion that you were under great stress because you lost your girlfriend and your father at the same time. Everyone believed that you became so depressed that you committed suicide, and your body was taken away by the ocean, never to be seen again."

I replied to Sharda, "I am sorry that I did not say goodbye or I did not tell you that I was leaving. Everything happened so fast. I managed to hitch hike on a ship that was leaving that night. When I left everyone was asleep, so I could not say goodbye. My journey was to Trinidad in search of my uncle whom I never knew I had, until my father told me just before his death. I promised my dad that I would find his brother. My mission was two-fold. One was to find my uncle, which I already accomplished. I am presently living in Trinidad with my uncle. The second mission was to find the one that I truly love, Monica. I am here to get information on her whereabouts which I hope you will provide me."

Sharda's next question to me was "Are you married?"

I replied "No."

She then continued, "Monica is living in United States. The last time I saw her was a year after she left for the United States. She came back to Guiana with the hope of reuniting and legally marrying you."

I then asked, "What happened to the boy whom Monica was supposedly engaged to?"

Sharda said that Monica never met him again because she deliberately traveled to United States on a later flight than planned so as to deceive everyone. Upon her arrival at the airport, no one was there to receive her. She walked around the airport wondering what to do next, and then she saw a nun and found the courage to approach her and asked for her help. The nun helped her and took her to live at her house, and she was still living with the nun when she came to Guiana.

Sharda then looked at me, smiled and said, "I have good news for you that I never told anyone else." I looked at her inquiringly; eagerly waiting for her to continue. She paused for a moment before saying, "Monica has a daughter." I looked at Sharda in astonishment wondering if Monica was married. Sharda then continued, "You found an uncle whom you never knew you had. Now I am happy to tell you that you have a daughter that you never knew you have. Monica was three months pregnant with your child before leaving Guiana. She did not tell anyone about her pregnancy when she departed to United States. Six months later she gave birth to a beautiful baby girl."

I got up placed the palm of my hand on my forehead and shouted "Oh god, Sharmila! Is it possible that Sharmila is my daughter and she was told that her dad is dead because everyone believed that I was dead?" I then paused for a moment and said, "No, it is not possible because Sharmila mom's name is Mona." Sharda then looked at me and said she did not know my daughter's name.

I explained to Sharda, "I met a teenage girl named Sharmila that resembled Monica so much so that I felt that Monica was in-front of me. I first met her when she was seven years old and I again met her a few weeks ago.

She spent a month's vacation with us and departed to United States a few days ago. She is the identical picture of Monica and is the same age as the last time I met Monica. I asked her about her parents, and she said that her mother's name is Mona and her father is dead. I had my doubts because whenever I looked at her I saw the resemblance of Monica. My doubts prompted me to be here today to get some answers. It would be the happiest day if Sharmila is my daughter."

Sharda then handed me an address for Monica that was given to her by Monica on her last trip to Guiana. I looked at the address and said to her, "I believe, I know the neighborhood of that address and as soon as I return to Trinidad, I will be on the next flight to United States."

Sharda said to me "You need a visa and money to go to United States"

I smiled and said to her, "There are many more surprises that I have for you. The first one is, I already have residency for United States and the second one is that I am not poor anymore. I will tell you more when I return to Guiana after finding Monica."

Sharda was surprised as she looked at me. I then asked for her husband, Jayboy. She answered that Jayboy was not at home. He became an alcoholic and whenever he got drunk, he talked non- stop about the two of us. I was always in his thoughts. Sharda continued that after I went missing, Jayboy never talked to Monica's parents again because he always blamed them for my disaster, and every time he saw them he swore at them.

I also found out that after I went missing, Jayboy became depressed and that was when he started to consume more liquor. Sharda told me that on some nights when he got too drunk, he slept at the downstairs of my house. I also learned that Sharda and Jayboy have three children (one boy and two girls). I got up and told Sharda that I was going to get Jayboy. Sharda then handed me a key for the house and she said she would accompany me.

We got into the taxi and drove a block to my house. As we arrived, we saw Jayboy was indeed sleeping on a hammock that was under the house. I walked towards him and woke him from his deep sleep. As he opened his eyes, he almost fell off the hammock as he stared at me in disbelief. He saw Sharda beside me, so he knew that he was not dreaming. He got up and hugged me as tears started to flow from his eyes.

After our emotional reunion, I went to meet the taxi driver and told him to pick me up about eight the following morning. I paid him generously as he said to me before departing, "See you in the morning". I took my bag and headed back to meet Sharda and Jayboy. We then went upstairs and Sharda lit a lamp as we sat and once again started our conversation. I questioned Jayboy about his drinking habits and his behavior. His excuse was that from the day I went missing and presumably dead, he blamed himself for not doing enough to help me overcome my difficult and stressful situation. He said that I helped him when he needed me, but he let me down when I needed his friendship the most. Liquor was the only thing that helped him to take away his sorrows.

I said to him, "Now you know that I am alive. Would you be a changed man?"

He got up from the hammock and told me that he would be back in a minute, as he went downstairs. He came back with a bottle of liquor and said, "I do not need this anymore," as he started to empty the bottle in the sink. He then went over to his wife and hugged her and said, "I am taking an oath in the presence of both of you that from now onwards I would no-longer consume liquor and I would be a dedicated husband and father to my wife and my children." He then went on to tell his wife how much he loved her.

It was after midnight as Jayboy and Sharda said good night to me. They were still holding hands as I watched them walk towards their house. I was so happy to know that they would once again be a happy family. I then took the lamp, walked around in the house. It was neatly kept but needed some repairs. I did not get a good look of the exterior because it was dark. I then went in the bedroom. The bed was neatly made. The shelf that I used for storing my clothes was still there. I placed my bag on the shelf then I noticed something on the shelf. As I unfolded it, to my surprise it was one of Monica's dresses and in it was a letter addressed to me. Monica deliberately left this dress with a note.

I opened the letter and to my surprise I found a picture of Monica and our baby when she was just born. In the letter she explained, "Everyone said that you are dead but I know deep down in my heart that you are alive and someday would return to me." She explained to me in the letter about her pregnancy with my child and apologized that she did not get the chance to tell me before she left Guiana. She wrote about how she conspired to evade the boy of her parents' choice. She told me about the nun that helped her. She ended by telling me how much she loved me and that she would be waiting for me. She left an address where I would find her. It was the same address that Sharda gave me. She signed her name with my last name (Monica Prashad.) At the bottom of the letter, she wrote, P.S. "I am leaving a picture of me and our daughter and please write me as soon as you get this letter. Until I hear from you, I would not step foot in Guiana."

I hung the dress on the bedroom wall and I read the letter a few times more as I lay on the bed staring at the picture. I kissed it and said, "I love you", as I placed the picture on my chest and fell asleep.

Early the following morning Jayboy and Sharda came over with my breakfast. Sharda made *rotie* with fried pumpkin and a cup of tea for me. She knew exactly what I loved for breakfast when I was a young boy growing up. After breakfast I showed them the letter and picture of Monica and my daughter. I asked them to promise me not to tell anyone that I found information on Monica.

We went downstairs around nine that morning and I could see the outside of the house and yard more clearly. The yard was well kept and Jayboy planted the garden. I saw many fruit trees at the backyard. The house needed many repairs. I also saw a "Property for Sale" sign on the next door neighbor's yard. I asked Jayboy who was the owner of that property.

He said "The original owner died and his son (Sham) inherited the property, but he has his own house, so he is selling this one. He lived in one of the neighboring village (Chesney Road) by the main public road."

I told them that I would buy that property and extend my house with two additional bedrooms and an upstairs verandah. Jayboy offered to take me to meet Sham.

As I looked across the street, I could see the taxi waiting for me. I asked Jayboy and Sharda to join me on my trip to New Amsterdam and they accepted my offer.

As we headed to the main road, Jayboy showed me Sham's home and I asked the chauffeur to stop. We were lucky because Sham was in his front yard as we approached him. I told him that I was interested in purchasing the property that was on sale. He accepted my proposal and I then finalized the deal to purchase the property. I took him to an attorney where we signed all the necessary documents and the purchase was legally finalized.

I then proceeded to New Amsterdam telecoms where I was able to make a phone call to Sita. She said that her father was sick and he was heading back to Trinidad in two days. As per his doctor's advice, he needed complete bed rest and he should consider retiring permanently. I promised Sita that I would return home the following day. She also asked me if I found any information on Monica and I answered, "I did." Without going into details I told her that I would tell her everything when I returned to Trinidad.

After I said goodbye to Sita, I phoned Raj. He was very happy to hear from me. I told him that I was in Guiana, and upon my return to Trinidad I would visit him in United States. He told me that for the past few days he was staying with his grandfather (Ram) because he was not feeling too well and that Ram would be traveling to Trinidad in two days. I told him that since Ram was traveling on Saturday, he should consider accompanying him on his trip back to Trinidad and spend the weekend with us. I then asked him "How is Sharmila?"

He said she was with him and continued to tell me that she still cannot get over her vacation to Trinidad. She wanted to talk to me so Raj gave her the phone and she said, "Dad, how are you? I missed you."

I answered, "I missed you too. I am in Guiana and I met two of my old friends. I would share some of the good news when I travel to United States in a couple of days."

We later went to a restaurant where we had lunch but before heading back home. I took Jayboy and Sharda to the bank where I opened a joint account between the two of them and myself .I then transferred a sum of money to be used for the renovation and extension of my house and I also gave them some money for themselves. We then went to Sharda's home where we spent the rest of the day with her family. I promised the children that I would help them, but they must promise me that they would attend high school and I would pay for their school fees. We later had an enjoyable dinner that was prepared by Sharda and I was very happy to see Sharda and Jayboy once again spending such an enjoyable time together. Jayboy again told me how happy he was to see me again, and he repeated that now that he knows that I am alive, his life would change forever.

As the place started to get dark, I headed home for an early night's rest because my flight back to Trinidad was scheduled to depart the following morning at eleven, so I had to leave home about five in the morning.

The following morning, I got out of bed around four. I saw the taxi was already outside waiting. Jayboy and Sharda came over around four-thirty. They joined me on my trip to the airport as we departed for our four hours' journey. We were on time at the airport. My plane was there already, so I said goodbye to Sharda and Jayboy, promising them that I would return soon and I hope that Monica would be with me when I return. They promised me that they would ensure that my house renovations would be completed in less than three months.

When I reached home Sita was waiting for me. She was very happy as I told her that I have some information about Monica's whereabouts and that I was hoping to find her on my next trip to United States. I did not tell her that I have a daughter. I wanted to surprise her when I have the reunion with Monica, hoping that she is still single and waiting for me as she mentioned in her letter.

Chapter 17
Ram's Retirement

A day after I returned from Guiana, Ram also returned from United States accompanied by Raj. Sita and I received them at the airport and as Ram walked toward me, I could not help but notice that he was pale and weak. He was eighty-two years old, so it was no surprise that old age started to take a toll on him. We hugged both of them as they boarded the car and started our homeward journey.

That evening during our family dinner, Ram told us that he was retiring permanently and asked me to take over the entire business. He said he knew that I was capable of handling all aspects of the business and he has full confidence in me. Sita and Raj also agreed with Ram's decision. Ram also told me that he had a very important meeting scheduled for next Wednesday in United States and he asked me to attend that meeting. After dinner he handed me a folder and said that all the documents were in the folder and he gave me the details. I spent the next two days with Ram and Raj and Sita before departing with Raj to the United States.

Sita knew that I wanted to go to United States as soon as possible to find Monica with the information that I received while in Guiana, so she told me "best of luck and I hope you achieve your dreams and find your lost love. I would be waiting for both of you when you return. It would be a joyous day for the entire family."

During our flight, I told Raj about my three days stay in Guiana. Raj was not aware that I was born in Guiana. He believed that I choose Guiana as one of my vacation destinations. He always thought that I lived all my life in Trinidad, so I did not tell him that I originally came from Guiana. I was waiting for the right time when I re-united with Monica to break the news to him and Sharmila. He believed that I went vacationing in Guiana so he asked me about my vacation. I told him that I met two friends and we spent some enjoyable time together. I also promised that I would take him and Sharmila on my next trip to Guiana. Raj answered that Sharmila would love to see where her parents were born. Her mom probably still has some family members who Sharmila had never met or heard of, because her mom never wanted to talk about her life in Guiana.

I then told Raj that I never met Sharmila's mom and I wanted to meet her some day. Raj replied that she is very pretty and a wonderful person, but she does not go to parties or social gathering. She only goes to work and back home. The only other places that she went were Sharmila's school events or meetings and she loves shopping. Raj promised that he would find the appropriate time to convince Sharmila's mother to meet me.

It was late in the night when we arrived in New York. Raj had parked his car at the airport so he drove me home to Long Island where he spent the night at our house and early the following morning drove to College. I then went in search of Monica. I had the address for her from the letter and from Sharda that she left while she was in Guiana.

I went to that address and knocked on the door. A lady opened the door; it was not Monica but I saw the resemblance of someone that I met somewhere. I asked her: "Anyone by the name of Monica lives here?"

Rather than answering my question, she looked at me for a few seconds and questioned. "Have we met before? Are you Raj's dad?"
I answered, "Yes."

She then said, "Please come in, and have a seat". She then continued, "We met about ten years ago. My name is Jessica".

At that point I recalled that she brought Sharmila to meet us at the beach when Raj was a little boy.

Jessica then asked, "What is your name? The last time we met I never asked you. I addressed you as Raj's dad."

I replied "My name is Ricky and I was given this address as the address for Monica. Do you know her?"

Jessica replied that she knew her and that Monica moved many years ago because they needed an additional bedroom as her daughter got older.

I then asked her "Were you a nun?"

She replied: "Yes".

At that point I was almost convinced that Sharmila is my daughter and her mother is Monica so I asked Jessica "Is Sharmila the daughter of Monica?"

Jessica then started telling me that Mona is Monica, and no one knew that she changed her name except her. Jessica said that she was happy to meet me because Monica told her all about our relationship. She then gave me her address and said that Sharmila probably already left for school. Her mom leaves for work around eight-thirty. She then wished me, "best of luck."

It was already eight-fifteen, so I drove as quickly as possible to the address that was given to me by Jessica. As I approached her house I realized that I was a little too late because I saw Monica joined the bus, so I drove following the bus driving closely, stopping behind the bus at all the stops looking to see if Monica was coming out.

As the bus arrived in Manhattan, it stopped in front of our warehouse building and to my surprise, I saw Monica then came out with a few other employees and they walked into the warehouse. I drove to the office, which was four buildings away from the warehouse, and phoned the manager of the warehouse and asked him if someone by the name of Mona worked there. He confirmed that she is an employee working for us.

I was very happy that after twenty years I finally will see Monica, but I was still anxiously waiting to be face to face with her. I told our office secretary, Sharon, that there is someone working in the warehouse that I wanted to hire as my personal secretary, and she should set up an interview with her in an hour. Her name is Mona and I told her that when Mona arrived to bring her in the conference room and place me on a conference call without her knowledge. During the interview I asked the secretary to ask her only two questions. The first question was if she used any other names. The second question was if she is married/divorce or single. If she answered that she is married, ask her for her husband's name. I did not want to confront Monica because I wanted to ensure that she did not remarry and also I wanted to surprise her.

Sharon came in my office about an hour later and told me that Mona was there. I told Sharon to take her in the conference room and I would be in my private room listening and joining her on her earpiece as she conducted the interview with Mona.

I could see Monica through a small glass that was on my office door as she was escorted into the conference room. After about five minutes, I phoned the secretary and asked her to place the call on speaker, which she did and I could hear Monica nervously talking to the secretary.

After offering her the new position, Sharon asked Mona the two questions that I told her to ask. Mona's answer was the same that I expected. Her other name is Monica and concerning the other question she answered that she is married and her husband's name is Ricky Prashad which is my full name and her answer confirmed that she never re-married.

I then joined in on the interview via speaker-phone. I told her that she was highly recommended for this new position that had opened in my office and I would like to offer her this new position. I continued to tell her that according to our records, she worked with our company for over eighteen years and I complemented her for her dedication. I told her that I considered her as a family member and she would be the best choice to be my assistant. Monica answered that she did not even have a high school certificate. I answered her that I knew that she did not have a high school certificate. All she would need to do is to take my messages and manage my appointments, and I am positive that she is capable of handling that task. I also told her that her salary would be doubled from what she is receiving presently.

After a lot of persuasion by Sharon, Monica finally accepted the position. I then asked my secretary to take her to her new office which is adjacent to mine. As they reached to her office door, Sharon said to her, "There is a box on your desk with stationery for you." Sharon then walked back to her desk as Mona walked in her new office, looking around, staring at the paintings on the wall. As she walked around her desk towards her chair ready to open the box, she noticed a frame with a picture of Raj and Sharmila on her desk which I had placed there earlier. She held it in her hand, surprised and baffled why that picture was there. She ran towards Sharon with the picture still in her hand and nervously asked her "Who put this picture on my desk?"
Sharon replied, "My boss placed it there for you. He met Raj and Sharmila and he knows that you will be happy to have that picture in your office."

Monica asked, "Who is your boss?"
Sharon answered, "I will tell you more about my boss after you settle down in your new office."

Sharon accompanied Mona back to her office; she showed Mona my office and told her, "This is the office of your boss. As soon as you finish packing, he would like to see you."

I was anxiously waiting for Monica, wondering what would be her reaction when she sees me. About fifteen minutes later, there was a knock on my door. It was Monica; she said, "This is Mona, can I come in?"

I answered "yes." As she opened the door and walked in, I deliberately went to the file cabinet by the wall, acting as if I was looking for documents, with my back facing her. I told her to have a seat, as I continued looking through the cabinet. I asked her if I could call her Monica instead of Mona and she approved. I then continued by asking her if she has a daughter named Sharmila and she answered "yes". I told her that I knew her daughter Sharmila and her boyfriend, Raj. They are like family members to me; I also said that I was born in British Guiana, and I knew her husband Ricky and her friends Sharda and Jayboy.

She nervously asked, "Who are you?"

I replied "You can consider me a family member," but before she could ask another question I told her "there is a gift bag on my desk. It is for you."

Monica then took the bag, opened it and took the gift out. As she looked at it, she realized it was the dress and a letter that she left for me in Guiana as a memory of her. She kept looking at the dress and letter wondering how I got them; but before she said another word, I answered, "While I was on vacation in Guiana, I was given this gift to deliver to you, but before I answer any other questions, can you please open the envelope on my desk? It has a few letters from someone who sent them to me and I want you to contact that person as your first task in your new position."

As Monica nervously opened the envelope and saw the letters, she yelled, "These are letters that I wrote. Ricky is that you?"

She started to cry as I told her, "Yes, it is me and I am alive, searching for you for the last eighteen years." I then turned and walked towards her. She looked at me, making sure that it was indeed me, and she then screamed, "Ricky!

You are alive" and she ran towards me, hugged me tightly as she continued to cry with joy. We continued hugging and kissing each other none-stop as tears flowed from our eyes. It was indeed an emotional reunion. I then looked at her and told her that I was searching for her for many years. I came to United States eleven years ago, inquired and searched the five boroughs for her. I was so close in finding her when Sharmila was seven years old and she spent a day with Raj, Sita and me. But because she changed her name, I did not realize that Mona was Monica.

Monica was surprised that I knew Raj and Sharmila but was baffled on my relationship with Raj and Sita, which prompted her to ask me if I was married to Sita and Raj is my son.

I told her that "I could never marry anyone else because she was always in my heart and the only one that I truly love. As for Sita, she is my cousin but I treated her as my sister. Raj is Sita's son, his father died when he was just two years old. I treated him as my own child and he even called me dad and respected me as his father. The handy work of God had brought Raj and Sharmila together, not realizing that Sharmila is my own daughter."

"After Sharmila visited us last summer, I saw the resemblance to Monica which prompted me to go to Guiana in search of information which I received from Sharda and resulted in me finding you, *my lost love.*"

Monica then complimented me on my looks. She said she never imagined seeing me so well dressed, wearing a suit and tie. She never saw me in such a good condition. She believed that I was one of the managers working in the office, so she asked me how I was able to get a manager's position and how long I have been working with that company because she never saw me around before.

I smiled as I continued hugging her then looked at her and I said: "There are many things that I need to tell you which I would go into detail another day but to make a long story short; I left Guiana, hitchhiked on a ship to Trinidad then I found my lost uncle who is a millionaire and owned many companies including the one where you work. I helped my uncle with his business. Now my uncle is retired. I became not a manager of this company, but I am the owner". I smiled as I continued: "My life had changed, from rags to riches. I am no longer that poor boy dressed in rags wondering about my next meals. I always followed my dad's advice to be loyal, honest, dedicated and helpful to others. Today that I found you my dreams are fulfilled."

Monica gasped with surprise upon hearing the good news; I told her that I was searching for her *across the oceans* for many years so that she could share my success. Now that I found her, I asked her, "Would you marry me legally immediately."

She replied, "Yes, let's do it right now. I waited eighteen years for this day and I cannot wait any longer".

I kissed her and said, "Let's go." We walked hand in hand. I introduced her as Monica and my wife to my secretary as she stared at us in surprise wondering what was going on. I told her that I would give her more details later and I asked her not to tell anyone else until I was ready to disclose my secret to the rest of our employees.

The first thing Monica and I did after leaving the office was to go the jewelry store for wedding rings which were chosen by Monica. We then headed straight to City Hall where we got married legally. I told Monica that I waited all my life for this day and I promised her that I would continue to love her as I did eighteen years ago and there is no one to stop us to continue from where we left off.

Monica replied that she returned to Guiana seventeen years ago with the intention of marrying me legally but everyone said that I was dead. She was the only one who believed that I was alive and she waited all those years with the hope of reuniting with me someday and now she is happy to say that her dreams were fulfilled.

We then drove to my house in Long Island, and as I stopped in-front our estate compound and opened the gate, Monica asked where we are going. I answered that we are going to our house. I could see how surprised Monica was as I stopped in-front the house as she looked at the huge, beautiful house with well-taken-care landscape. I gave her a tour of the house, and we spent the rest of the day catching up from where we left off years ago. It was indeed a special romantic reunion.

As evening came upon us, Monica said that it was getting late and it was time for her to go home. She continued that she was always home to welcome Sharmila when she returned from school and this would be the first time that she was not home when Sharmila arrived. I told her that this is her new home and they should move in as soon as possible; and we need to figure how we are going to break the news of our relationship to both Sharmila and Raj. I am almost positive they would both be happy because they considered me as their dad in their own ways; but we should wait to tell them at the most appropriate time.

Monica then phoned Sharmila and told her that she is out with a childhood friend and that she would be late. Sharmila was surprised because her mom never stayed out late, but she was happy that for the first time her mom was out with a friend enjoying herself so she said to Monica to take her time and not to rush home and for her to have an enjoyable time.

Monica and I later had a candle light dinner together that was prepared by Monica. Her home cooking food brought back memories of the days when I used to enjoy her meals. I complimented her and said, "This is the best meal that I had in eighteen years."

After dinner and a romantic day, I drove Monica home and told her that I would pick her up the following morning. Sharmila did not see me when we arrived because I drove off as soon as Monica opened the door to her apartment. Sharmila was up waiting for her mom and hugged her as she entered their apartment. She could see the happiness in her mom's face even before her mom told her that she spent one of the best days after many years. Sharmila then asked her mom that she would like to meet her friend some day, to which Monica replied, "Yes."

Chapter 18
Major Announcement

The following morning I went in Monica's apartment for the first time. Although it was neatly kept, I was shocked to see how small it was. It had two small bedrooms, a small living room, and no walls separating the kitchen. Monica made breakfast for us which was *rotie* (pita bread) with fried vegetables. I once again enjoyed her delicious cooking. After lunch I took her shopping to some of the best name brands store. She was hesitant at first when she saw the prices but I told her that it was time for her to have a new wardrobe and not to look at the prices. I convinced her that she is now my legally married wife and it's time for her to enjoy my success.

After shopping, I dropped her home before heading to a meeting that was scheduled prior by Ram. I later went to the office where I spent an hour before heading back to Monica's apartment where I spent the rest of the afternoon but I left before Sharmila returned from school.

Later that evening I told Raj that I was planning to invite Sharmila and her mother to spend the weekend with us, and he should make all the necessary arrangements to pick them. Raj loved my plan but was skeptical whether Sharmila's mom would attend because she never goes out to parties or social occasions.

My reply to Raj was that I am positive I would able be to convince her to attend, and he should plan to be there. I then phoned Monica and told her about my plans and we should be prepared to tell Sharmila and Raj the truth about our relationship.

The following Morning, which was on a Thursday, Raj phoned me and said that he was surprised that Sharmila and her mom would be joining us on Saturday and he wondered how I managed to convince her to attend. I told him that I planned more surprises when we get together.

Later that day I arranged with my secretary to inform the warehouse manager that Mona has been promoted to a new position as an office secretary. She would be visiting the warehouse later in her new capacity along with another employee. The secretary did not disclose my identity because no one from the warehouse had ever met me. I also informed the secretary to order lunch on behalf of Monica for all the warehouse employees and she should arrange with our regional director to attend this luncheon and introduce me.

I dressed with ordinary clothes (no suit or tie) because I did not want the warehouse employees to know my identity until later that day as I wanted to get a first hand experience of the entire operations.

When Monica and I arrived at the warehouse, we were met by the manager who congratulated Monica on her promotion. She then introduced me as an employee. All other employees also congratulated her on her promotion as we walked through the different departments, and the managers informed them about Monica's promotion. As we arrived at the department where Monica was working, it was indeed an emotional moment as I watched Monica and her coworkers exchanged hugs and congratulations. I continued my tour to the shipping department where I spent about two hours, assisting other employees before being joined by Monica.

We all gathered for lunch in the lunchroom and were joined later by my secretary and regional manager. After lunch the regional manger told the employees that there were two major announcements that he wanted to announce. "The first one is that Mona would no longer be working in the warehouse because she was promoted as personal secretary to the President and owner of the company. The second announcement is that Ram has retired and the new owner is his son, Ricky who is with us here today." He then pointed to me and said, "Here is Ricky."

I stood up and told the workers that "it was a pleasure spending a few hours with everyone and I am impressed by their dedication. The reason why I did not disclose my identity was because I wanted all employees to consider me as one of them and my office is always open for them". I also told them that "there would be no changes and every thing would remain the same as it was under Ram. As for Mona, I wish to inform everyone that she is not only my personal secretary but a co-owner of our company because she was my childhood girl friend and is now my wife and her real name is Monica." Everyone was caught by surprise on the announcement, and they once again congratulated Monica as she assured them that her friendship for them would not change and they should still consider her as an employee. She hugged everyone before the two of us left for the day.

Chapter 19
Sharmila and Raj learned the truth

Raj normally spends the weekend with me at our house in Long Island, so he picked up Sharmila and her mom on Saturday morning and brought them over. This was the first time that Sharmila came to our house in Long Island. She also thought that it was the first time that her mom came here, not knowing that she had already visited me.

Sharmila visited our home in Trinidad; so when they arrived, she was not too surprised to see our beautiful estate. I was outside waiting for them. I hugged Sharmila and told her that I missed her. Her mom then came over hugged me and gave me a kiss as Sharmila looked in surprise at her mom. Raj took Sharmila for a tour of the house as Monica and I spent some time discussing the agenda for the day and planned our move to confront the kids with the truth.

Within a short time Raj and Sharmila returned and joined us as we started to barbeque. Monica requested that she would cook the meals, assisted by our cook.

While Monica was preparing some delicious meals, Sharmila once again looked at her and was baffled to see how comfortable and happy her mom was.

It was a beautiful day as we sat at the back porch facing the pool with the water fall and lovely flowers in the background, as we sipped on some wine and ate some snacks as we listened to Sharmila talking about her vacation to Trinidad and the wonderful time she had. She then talked about her mom; and for the first time, she saw how happy her mom was. Sharmila then asked me about my trip to Guiana. I told her that while I was in Guiana, I met two of her Mom's friends and they gave me many details about her mom.

Sharmila interrupted by saying that her mom doesn't talk about her life in Guiana, and she would like to hear the details.

I then looked at Monica and said to Sharmila, "As I told you on the phone while I was in Guiana, I received information about your mom and dad." Your mom knew your dad since she was a child. They were childhood friends. As they grew older, they were deeply in love and they became romantically involved. Their problem started when your mom's parents found out about their affairs. Your dad's parents came from a poor family, whereas your mom's parents were wealthy, so they disapproved of your parents' relationship. They did everything in their power to separate your parents but were unsuccessful. So they had your dad arrested on prompt-up charges."

I could see the sadness on Sharmila's face as I continued. "While your dad was detained, your grandparents forcibly engaged your mom to someone else and sent her to the United States. She never told anyone that she was pregnant with your dad's child. After your dad was released and all charges were dismissed and he went home, he found that his father suffered a heart attack and he died a few days later. Your mom never married anyone else, and after your birth, she went back to Guiana to marry your dad legally but she was told that he died by committing suicide.

I could see tears flowing from both Sharmila and her mom's eyes. Sharmila then asked me to tell her more about her father. I walked over to her and held her in my arms and told her. "I have some news about your dad. He never committed suicide as everyone believed. He is alive and was searching for your mom for the past eighteen years. He left Guiana traveling *across the oceans in search of his lost* love not knowing that he also has a daughter"

Sharmila then asked, "Where is my dad? I am dying to meet him! Although I have always looked upon you I as my dad, and you will always be my dad; no one can replace you but I would like to meet the man that my mother always kept in her memory since I knew her."

I hugged Sharmila tightly, looked into her eyes and said, "You already met your dad."

Sharmila looked baffled as she asked "When and where?"

I continued by telling her, "your dad hitch-hiked on a ship which was heading for Trinidad where he lived for many years until he finally traveled to United States. He searched for his love (your mom) but without success because she changed her name from Monica to Mona. Your dad met his daughter twice when she was seven years old and again when she was seventeen years old without knowing that he had a child, until he went to Guiana and learned the truth from your mom's friend, Sharda."

Sharmila looked at me and started to cry again as she pointed at me and said "You?"

I answered, "Yes, I am your dad and your mom's real name is Monica and she is my wife."

Sharmila hugged me tightly as she said, "This is the best gift that I ever had in my entire life." She then looked at Raj and said to me, "If I am your daughter and Raj is your son. That makes us brother and sister."

Raj then answered. "There is another secret that I would disclose. My real dad's name is Rohan. He died when I was a child. I grew up with your dad as my own dad. He was there for me as a child and always treated me as his own son, and I would always consider him as my own dad."

I then went on to tell Sharmila that Raj's father rescued me in Trinidad; and after his death in an accident, I found out that Raj's grandfather is my adopted Uncle, and the person that I came to Trinidad in search of after my father's death. While in Trinidad, I also gained the sisterly love of Ram's daughter, Sita. I gained a sister that I never had before. Ram took me in as his own son and gave me everything including his business. He said he is indebted to my grandparents and my dad for adopting him when he was an orphan and nothing could repay the love he received from them. I then hugged Raj and Sharmila; and said to them that I am proud to have both of them as my children.

I could see that Monica was sobbing, so I went over and hugged her telling her, "Today we are united as a family. We gained not only a son and a daughter but a sister and a father. Today is a joyous day and we should enjoy it as a new starting point as a family." Raj and Sharmila came over to me and Monica then hugged us. It was indeed an emotional moment as the four of us joyfully hugged each other.

We spent the rest of the day having an enjoyable time as we munched on the delicious dishes prepared by Monica. I later phoned Sita. The first question she asked me, if I found Monica. I said that I not only found Monica, but also a daughter that I recently learned that I had. Sita said that she cannot wait to meet both Monica and our daughter. I told her that she already met them. I then told her that Sharmila is my daughter and Mona is Monica and the one that I was searching for the last nineteen years.

She was overjoyed to receive this good news. She said that she already had a good relationship with both Monica and Sharmila and was happy to hear that they are part of the family, and she cannot wait for a reunion. She then asked me to bring them as early as possible to Trinidad.

Nightfall came upon us as we were having an enjoyable time. Monica said that it was getting late, and it was time to go home. I said to her, "This is your home and this is where you and Sharmila would live as of today." I also asked Raj not to stay at the dorm anymore, but to move here permanently; and Sharmila and him should consider getting married as soon as possible. Raj replied that they already decided that they would get married in the summer. I was very happy to hear the good news as we continued to enjoy spending the first evening as a family before going to bed.

The following day was a Sunday. I phoned Jessica and invited her for dinner; I told her that Mona and Sharmila would also be with Raj and me. She was happy that Mona would be present and promised that she would join us after church.

Monica and I wanted to give Jessica the good news about our reunion and to thank her for her assistance. I sent Raj to pick her up because she never came to our house before. As Jessica arrived, she was also surprised to see where we lived; and she said to me that she was impressed to see how humble we were.

Monica welcomed Jessica and escorted her into the house where we sat on the sofa and started to chat.

I arranged prior with Monica that she should break the news to Jessica about our relationship, so as soon as Monica found the opportunity, she told Jessica that she wanted to share some good news with her. Jessica looked at her and said she was dying to hear the news. Monica said, "The good news is after many years; I found my love that I was waiting to meet and be reunited again someday." She continued that she would like to introduce her husband and the father of Sharmila. She then told Jessica that I am her husband and the one that she was waiting for many years. Jessica knew that I went to search for Monica but was still surprised and happy as she hugged both of us. We then thanked her for everything she had done to help Monica and her daughter. Monica then told her that she would use her real name, Monica as of that day.

Jessica was also surprised when she learned that Monica was working with our company. She said, "When Monica came to United States, Ram helped her by giving her a job when she was desperately in need of it. This is the handy work of the lord that set the stage for this happy day."

Later that evening after Jessica left, I received a call from Jayboy and Sharda who told me that the renovation of my house in Guiana was completed and they also added a beautiful design fence around the property, Jayboy then asked me if I found Monica. I replied that I did and that

Sharmila is indeed my daughter. I told him that we were planning to return to Guiana for our marriage reception on December 23, and he should start making preparations. I also asked him to demolish the house that I bought next door, and he could use the materials to repair their house and use the open space to build a shed.

For the next few days I spent some wonderful time with my newfound family and I enjoyed every moment of it. Monica and I continued our relationship from where we left off. The only difference now is that we can afford many more things that we couldn't when we were in Guiana. I now felt as if I was once again re-living my dreams with Monica.

As summer vacation arrived and Raj and Sharmila were off from school, we traveled to Trinidad where for the first time we were greeted as a family by Sita and Ram.

Sita threw a grand reception for us and for the first time introduced Monica as my wife. I was also surprised when she also announced the engagement of Raj and Sharmila. They kept their planned engagement a secret from Monica and me so as to once again give me another surprise.

Ram gave a touching speech as he complimented my parents and me. He talked about our relationship and how happy he was, ever since he met me. He said his days are numbered' and he was happy that Raj and Sharmila would be together to carry on our family legacy.

Sita also commented about gaining a sister-in-law whom she considered as a sister from the first time she met Monica twelve years ago and not forgetting Sharmila whom she always considered as a daughter. She thanked me for being there as her brother and showered her with brotherly love and affection.

Rose was also at the reception. I introduced her to Monica as a family friend, and she told Monica how happy she was to learn that at last I found the one that was always in my heart and the one that I was thinking about every day in hope of finding someday. Rose then introduced me to one of her childhood friends, Rakesh. She said that he lived in England, and he asked for her hand in marriage, which she accepted and was planning to get married and move to England. I complimented her and also thanked her for being a true friend for me who was always there to cheer me up when I needed it most. I then wished her all the best.

After the party, I spent the next few months traveling back and forth between Trinidad and the United States with most of my time in Trinidad being with my family as we visited numerous sight seeing, beaches and on one occasion we traveled to the Bahamas for three days, enjoying the beautiful landscape with its exquisite white- and pink-sand beaches, and its lush tropical trees and sunshine. I enjoyed walking with Monica along the beaches with its blue water splashing against our feet as we looked at the flying fish emerging from the water and looking like little planes as they landed.

At home Monica spent most of her time with Sita. Their relationship was very strong as they did many things together especially shopping and charitable work. Monica felt at home and considered Ram as her father and assisted Sita in taking care of him as he struggled through his old age.

Before the big day approached for our reception in Guiana, Monica and Sita did most of the shopping for this occasion and shipped a few boxes to Sharda in preparation for this special day. I also shipped one of our cars with the same ship that brought me to Trinidad. The captain and staff still have good relationship with me as we continued doing business with them for our import/export company. The car was for us to use while we are in Guiana.

Chapter 20
Trip to India

Monica and I continued spending more time with Ram during his retirement. I happened to notice that Ram sometimes stared in space as if his thoughts were somewhere else.

One day when Ram and I were alone, I decided to question him about my observation, and he confided in me, seeing how happy Monica and I were together after we were reunited. He was very happy for us and he wished that he would also reunite with his sister. He continued, "When I was busy working, I was concentrating on my business; but now that I am retired, I have more time to reflect on my early childhood days and I wish some day to see my birth place in India and reunite with my sister and her family once more before I leave this world." He also mentioned how much he missed his wife, Radica.

I discussed with Sita and Monica about Ram's wish and suggested to them that we should consider taking him for a vacation to India. In fact, I told them that we should make this trip with the entire family to search for our ancestors and possible reunite with them while Ram is still alive. Both Sita and Monica agreed that we should make the trip during this summer vacation. I also discussed our plan with Raj and Sharmila and they were excited to take this trip as they were on summer break.

I then communicated our plan to Ram who was very happy to take us to the Village where he grew up as a child to meet his sister that he hadn't seen for about sixty-seven years and he hoped that she was still alive. He also wanted to search for his wife's (Radica) family and give them the news about her being kidnapped and taken away to Trinidad. I was also excited to meet the aunt whom I never knew I had before my father's death; and I also wanted to see where my father spent his childhood days.

Ram was a very popular businessman and was well known throughout Trinidad. He had a good relationship with the Indian ambassador, so it was very easy for him to ask and receive assistance in obtaining visas, arranging transportation and assistance with accommodations while in India.

During the next few days, Sita and Monica were busy doing shopping for our trip while Ram and I visited the Trinidadian registration office where archived information on the immigrant was kept. Ram had Radica's birth certificate and he knew the ship they came with to Trinidad; so we managed to obtain information on Ram's wife, Radica, very easily. We found information on the Village she was born, her parents' names, their address and even her uncles and aunts' names. Ram said he was looking forward to meeting his wife's family and giving them details of Radica.

On the day of our trip to India, we boarded BWIA Airline enroute to London connecting to India. It was a long journey and we slept most of the trip to London where the plane stopped for refueling, dropped off and picked up additional passengers before continuing to India.

Almost twenty-four hours after leaving Trinidad, we landed in India about eight o'clock in the morning; and after collecting our baggage, we had breakfast at the airport terminal then proceeded to our awaiting transportation that was pre-arranged by the Indian Ambassador in Trinidad. We had a tour guide from the Indian ministry of tourism and also security was assigned for us.

The first place Ram wanted to visit was the Port of Calcutta, the last place he was in India before he boarded the ship. We traveled to Calcutta harbor and Ram proceeded toward the building as we followed him. He led us into the port and he stood by the dock gazing across the river then pointed to buildings across the river and said. "That building was the last place I was held for days with other immigrants about sixty-five years ago by the notorious system known as indentured servitude before boarding the ship to an unknown destination which I later found out was Trinidad." Ram then clasped his hand and said a prayer for those that lost their lives during the trip and at the hands of the cruel sugar estate owners and managers.

We then drove through the city of Calcutta that was very old and unsanitary. As we passed through the market square, people lined the street corners, some eating from leaves sitting on the ground, others cooking, selling live fowls, and slaughtering and cleaning lamb. The place was so filthy that we did not even want to eat the fresh fruits that were being sold in the market. We then drove to the railroad station for our journey to Bihar.

At the station we visited a coffee shop where we had our lunch before boarding the train.

We were lucky to be in a carriage for executive class passengers. It was a long journey, passing through small villages and farmlands before we reached the main city of Bihar known as Patna where we visited the office of the Minister of Bihar who was expecting us. He took us to a guesthouse where he arranged for us to stay while we were in Bihar. He also provided security and other means of transportation as we drove to the neighboring village of Muzaffarpur, which was the village of Ram's birthplace.

We drove through the streets of Muzaffarpur, passing small mud plastered houses with straw roofs and large farmlands. People stood by the street corners looking at us wondering who were visiting their village because they were not accustomed seeing vehicles in that area. As we passed the house where Ram's grandparents were living, he stopped the vehicle and showed us the house before driving to the house where he grew up as a child and where my father was born. Ram stepped out of the vehicle, touched the ground. We followed him as he stood and stared at the small trash house, and tears started to flow from his eyes. I started to get emotional also as I hugged Ram and told him how happy I was to be at the birthplace of my dad.

We walked to the house as people started to gather. I saw some one come out of the house, stand by the door as Ram walked towards him, and asked him his name. He said his name is Sewkumar. Ram then asked him his parents' name. I saw fear in his eyes as he nervously answered that his mother's name is Rukmin and his father name was Ramgolam. Ram then hugged him telling him, "My name is Ramoutar. I am your uncle and this is the house where I grew up. Where is your mother? I am dying to meet my sister."

Sewkumar answered that his father died about four years ago and his mother lived a block away with his younger brother. He also said that his mother told him that she has two brothers who went to a foreign land and never returned. She talked constantly about Ramoutar and Ramessar.

Ram then asked if he could take a tour of the house. Sewkumar took us in the house, called his wife, and introduced Ram as his uncle. He expressed his apology for not having any seats for us to sit. He pulled a cot and offered us a seat. He then asked his wife to prepare meals for us. Ram told him that some water would be fine.

We sat on the cot, while Ram sat on the floor as he did when he was a child. We sipped our drinks as Sewkumar told us about my aunt and the struggle she went through before he grew up and assisted his parents. He said that after Ram and his brother left, his father took care of the farmlands until Sewkumar was married and moved in the house, and he took over the responsibilities. Ram then toured the house and showed us where they slept. We walked to the back of the house, and Ram showed us the farm where they worked. He walked under a tree and showed us the spot that he and his brother played.

We then walked through the farmland looking at the different types of vegetables that were ready to be cultivated, before we headed back to the house where Ram told

Sewkumar that he wanted to do a religious ceremony on the soil where he and his brother grew up and he should consult a priest for Saturday and invite the entire Village for this occasion. Sewkumar looked at Ram in astonishment wondering where he would get the money to do the function. Ram told him not to worry about the cost, as he took a large sum of money and handed it to Sewkumar.

We then traveled a block to the house where my aunt Rukmin lived, accompanied by Sewkumar. We were very nervous as we walked in the yard to the door as Sewkumar opened it and went in. He called his mom and told her that he had a surprise for her as we stood at the opened door waiting. Rukmin slowly walked to the door as Ram stared at her emotionally. Tears of joys started to flow from his eyes as Rukmin asked, "Who are these people?"

Ram replied, "Do you have any brothers?"

Rukmin replied, "I have two brothers named Ramoutar and Ramessar. They went to a foreign land and never returned. I missed them very much. Do you know where they are?"

Ram started to cry as he told Rukmin, "Yes, I know your brothers. Ramessar died in a country called British Guiana and this is his son, Ricky" I extended my hand and held my aunt, hugged her and told her that I knew that my dad's spirit is looking down on us.

Rukmin then asked "Where is my other bother Ramoutar?"

I answered, "Your brother, Ramoutar is standing in-front of you"

Rukmin stared at Ram and said "Ramoutar, is that you?"

Ram answered, "Yes, I am your brother Ramoutar" as he hugged her and both of them tightly held each other with tears flowing from their eyes. Rukmin then held his hand as she led us in the house. They both kept looking at each other still holding each other's hands as Ram told her about his life after he left India. She was very happy to meet the entire family.

While Ram and Rukmin were catching up, we toured the farmlands at the back of the house accompanied by Sewkumar. I saw a man working in the farms. Sewkumar called him over and introduced him as his brother, Narine. He was very happy to meet his family that he never knew he had. He heard from his mom about Ramoutar and Ramessar. I told him that his uncle Ramoutar is in the house with his mom. Narine ran towards the house to meet his lost uncle who he heard so much about from his mom.

We decided that we would have a family get together for dinner so Monica and Sita went with Rukmin and her two daughters-in-law to the market and store where they bought ingredients to cook for dinner while Narine got vegetables from his garden. Sita prepared the meals and Monica assisted the daughters-in-law.

For the first time the entire family sat and had a hearty meal together while all the questions Rukmin had, were answered. Ram also asked Rukmin and her family to join us in Trinidad for a vacation and to be a part of my wedding celebration in British Guiana. They willingly agreed and Ram told them that he would take them the following day to the Embassy in India where they would get their visas.

After a wonderful family reunion, we went sight seeing around the Village. Ram showed us the different areas he spent during his childhood days. He showed us where his biological parents lived before their deaths, and the place he was born. He showed us the school he attended and many of the areas Ramessar and him spent time playing. We later said goodnight to Rukmin and family before heading to the guesthouse that was provided for us.

The following morning Ram and I took Rukmin and her children to the embassy in the City where they obtained their visas. We then went shopping where Ram bought beautiful saris, necklaces and bangles for Rukmin. He also bought many different types of clothes for Sewkumar and Narine.

Before we headed back to Rukmin's home, Ram, bought plane tickets for them to travel to Trinidad.

We spent the next three days preparing for Ram's religious function. Some of the neighbors helped built a huge bamboo tent. Rukmin's daughters-in-law did most of the preparation for the food; and as the day approached for the function, a group of musicians from the Mandir came over with their musical instruments, hand drums, *harmonium*, *dantals* and other instruments. They sang beautiful religious songs, joined by Rukmin and Ram. By the time the priest arrived, the yard was filled with villagers. Ram and Rukmin took part in the ceremony. The priest did a wonderful sermon and thanked Ram for remembering his birthplace and most importantly returning and performing a religious ceremony on the soil where he was born. After the ceremony everyone had delicious meals and Ram gave gifts to the elderly. The musicians played music and sang beautiful songs until late in the night.

Two days later with mixed emotions, we bade farewell to our new found family, telling them that we would meet again in a couple of months when they travel to Trinidad. Our next destination was Utter Pradesh in search of Radica's parents. We took the train back to Calcutta where we went to the minister's office who helped obtain information and an updated address for Radica's parents. We found out that her mother's name is Ratnie and her father name is Mohabir. They lived in a village called Allahabad, and Mohabir is a popular businessman.

We continued our journey from Calcutta to Utter Pradesh, passing trough many small villages before reaching the city, Lucknow, a business district of Utter Pradesh. Ram decided to buy gifts for Radica's family. We drove looking at the different stores deciding which one to go in. Ram pointed at a Sari store named "Radica Sari and Jewelry." He said that it would be a tribute to Radica buying gifts for her family from a store with her name.

We parked our vehicle and proceeded in the store. The sales man was very courteous, showing us the different clothes. Sita selected couple of different types of Saris, a few Jewelries and Kurtas. She then proceeded to the cashier at the checkout counter. The cashier kept staring at her, making Sita very uncomfortable. Ram noticed and walked up to the counter, looked at the cashier and then he noticed at the back of the counter, at the back wall was a shelf. On it was a picture frame of a girl with a garland around it and incenses burning in front. The picture looked like a photo of his wife, Radica when he first met her. Ram then asked the cashier "Who is the girl in the picture?"

The cashier answered: "That girl was my aunt. I was told that she is dead and my grandfather named this store Radica Sari and Jewelry in her memory. I saw the resemblance of your daughter to her. That is the reason I was staring at her. My name is Bharrat and I am the manager"

Ram then asked. "What is Radica's parents' name?"
Bharrat replied. "Her father's name is Mohabir and her mother's name is Ratnie. They are my grandparents and the owners of this store."

Ram became very emotional because he knew that Mohabir and Ratnie were Radica's parents; and he asked Bharrat if he could take a look at the picture. He took Ram to the picture. It was indeed a picture of Ram's wife, Radica when he first met her.

Ram took a flower that was placed at Radica's feet, clasped his hands with the flower in them and started praying. With tears in his eyes, he placed the flower on top the picture, and then kissed it as Bharrat was surprised wondering what was going on. Ram then turned to Bharrat, pointed to the picture and said, "That was my wife." He then pointed to Sita and said, "That is Sita, the daughter of Radica." Bharrat hugged Ram, then walked to Sita and hugged her.

Ram showed Bharrat the address that he had for Radica's parents and he confirmed that it was correct. We then proceeded to Allahabad and traveled to Radica's parents' address. They had a huge house with a beautiful painted fence and a beautiful flower garden in the yard. We stopped in front the house and proceeded into the yard. I rang the doorbell and a girl came to the door, inquiring how she could help us. Ram asked if Ratnie lived there, and she answered, "Yes" as she called, "Grandma, someone is here to see you."

We saw Ratnie as she walked to the door and asked, "Who are you?" Before I answered, she saw Sita and said "*Beti* (girl) come here." She kept staring at Sita and said to her, "You looked like my daughter, Radica who was missing many, many years ago. She would be seventy- eight years now."

Sita answered, "I looked like your daughter, Radica, because she is my mother and I am your granddaughter. I came from a country called Trinidad where your daughter was forcibly taken by notorious immigrant recruiters' and was taken on a ship and sent to Trinidad to work in the sugar estate where she lived until her death." Ratnie started to cry, hugged Sita, and invited us in the house.

The house was beautiful with expensive furniture. Sita introduced us and Ratnie called her husband, Mohabir, and gave him the news about Radica's whereabouts after she went missing. They said everyone believed that Radica was killed and her corpse was disposed of never to be found. They were curious to learn more about Radica's plight, and Ram started to tell them how he met Radica on the ship and helped her throughout the journey. "When we arrived in Trinidad, she was sent to work in the sugar-cane fields. She cried for days as I comforted her. She only trusted me and told me how she was kidnapped and was warned if she told anyone that she was forcibly placed on the ship that her entire family would be killed." Ram continued that they later got married and after indenturship was abolished, they started their own business and became very popular. "Radica lived like a princess with maids and servants. She was overjoyed when Sita was born. We lived happily until her death." Ram then showed them pictures of Radica at different ages and pictures of Radica and Sita as she was growing up. He also showed them pictures of their marriage. Ratnie and Mohabir were also overjoyed to meet their great-grandson, Raj.

That evening the entire family was invited for dinner and we were introduced to them. Mohabir said that he wanted us to stay with them for our entire vacation in Allahabad, which we did and for the next couple of days, we were taken sight seeing by one of Radica's brother.

Ram was happy when he visited the Holy Rivers--Ganga, Yamuna and Saraswatie--where he did some prayers for his ancestors. We also toured the business of Mohabir and Ratnie. They had three stores being managed by their sons and also a sewing factory where *saris*, *langas* and *Kurtas* were manufactured.

We spent three days with our new-found family before departing to Trinidad. Before we left Ram invited them to our marriage reception, and they promised that they would join us and they would keep in contact after we exchanged phone numbers. Ram also gave them his address. It was an emotional goodbye as we boarded the plane. During our flight we had many things to talk about. I never saw Ram so happy before our trip to India. When we reached home, the first thing Ram did was to go in-front his wife's picture and prayed, telling her that her dreams were now fulfilled and her family learned the truth, and most importantly, her family was reunited and her legacy would be carried on.

Chapter 21
Marriage Celebration

As December arrived, Monica and I decided to travel to Guiana three weeks prior to our reception date. The arrangement was that Raj and Sharmila would join us as soon as school closed for Christmas recess; and because we were expecting other family members from India, Sita and Ram would wait for them and join us three days prior to the celebration.

Monica and I departed to Guiana on the morning of December 2nd. Sharda had arranged with the taxi driver that I used when I last visited Guiana to pick us up at the airport.

Upon arrival in Guiana, Jayboy and Sharda were there to greet us. They were overjoyed to see Monica and me together, so much so that they could not hold back the tears of happiness. As soon as we cleared customs, Sharda ran towards Monica, grabbed her, and hugged her tightly with tears still flowing from her eyes with emotions. It's been almost eighteen years since they last met, and she always wished to see this day when Monica and I would be together.

We later joined the taxi to Georgetown with Monica and Sharda, catching up on old times; and Jayboy and I talking about the plan for our reception.

In Georgetown we dropped off to pick up my car, which we used for transportation to continue our journey to Kilcoy settlement. It was around one in the afternoon as we arrived and drove in our block towards our house. This was the first time since I left Guiana that I actually visited on a weekend. The last time I was in Guiana, it was during the weekdays when most people were at work or school, and I was out of the Village from morning until night, so people were not aware that I was in Guiana. This time it was different. I arrived when it was day and on a weekend when most people were at home.

As we drove through our street with the windows down in a luxurious car, people could not help but gaze at us in surprise. Those that recognized and knew us waved as we drove by, and many of them followed the car to our house to make sure it was me because everyone thought I was dead.

I stopped the car in-front of my house, and stepped out followed by Monica. Everyone was surprised not only in seeing that I was alive but also seeing Monica and me together. It was an emotional day as friends and neighbors greeted and hugged us. As we walked in the yard, Jayboy and Sharda took our suitcases in the house while Monica and I proceeded to the bottom of the house, followed by our neighbors who had many questions concerning my whereabouts and my reunion with Monica. I briefly told them that I hitch-hiked from Guiana to Trinidad, then traveled to United States where Monica and I reunited. I also invited them to join us in celebrating our wedding reception on December 23.

I spent about an hour chatting with my neighbors before I managed to take a tour of all the renovations that were done to the house.

The house was enclosed by beautiful fences and well decorated gates. The house looked huge from the outside with beautiful colored paints. The balcony upstairs was an eye catcher with its designed iron works. The stairs was moved from the outside to under the house with its sides enclosed.

Monica and I then proceeded upstairs where we were once again surprised to see the beautiful painted colors and decorations. We then toured the bedrooms. Instead of two, we now have four beautiful decorated bedrooms.

The kitchen was remodeled with new cabinets and sink. I then thanked Jayboy and Sharda for the good job they had done as we walked to the balcony where I spent the rest of the afternoon, relaxing and enjoying the beautiful view with Monica sitting beside me as we waved at people passing by, greeting us. We talked about some of the memorable times we had while living in Guiana until late into the night before we said goodnight to Jayboy and Sharda and then went to bed.

After breakfast the following morning, Monica and I went for a walk before stopping at Sharda's house where we met her children and spent some time with them.

As we were leaving Sharda's house, we saw Monica's parents, (Mohan and Anjee) in their backyard watering plants. They looked very old and frail. Sharda told me that they lived all by themselves. Their son moved to Georgetown and hardly visited them. Their other daughter, Chandra, never visited them since she eloped with her then boyfriend. Mohan and Anjee made their living by selling produce they reaped from their garden. Sharda said that some days things were so bad with them that she gave them some groceries. They are now in worse condition than what I experienced when I was living in Guiana. I felt pity for them as we headed home, not knowing if they saw us or even recognized us.

While Monica and I were sitting on our board hammock, which was under our house, we were surprised to see Sharda with Monica parents heading to our house. They stopped in front the gate and Sharda asked, "Can I bring them in?"

I looked at Monica and said "Yes."

As Monica parents walked slowly toward us, I could not believe my eyes to see those same people who used to have so much pride because of the position they held at their work place and the money they had. At that time they considered the poor as not being worthy to associate with. They trampled upon those that were poor, including me.

As I looked at Monica's parents shaggily dressed, I couldn't help feeling sorry for them as they stood in front of us. Monica's father then clasped his hand as if praying and said, "Please find it in your heart to forgive us. I know we had done many bad things to both of you because we had too much pride at the time. I beg you to please forgive us."

I looked at Monica as she answered, "As I said to you eighteen years ago when I last visited Guiana, the only way I will forgive you is, if Ricky first forgives you." I then got up and hugged both of them and told them that I forgave them. Monica also hugged them and forgave them. We then took them upstairs in our house and treated them with gifts and I asked them to spend the rest of the day with us because we had a lot to catch up.

Monica prepared lunch for us, and during our meals, I told her parents about our planned marriage reception and I asked them to be part of this ceremony. I also told them that they would be surprised to meet some of our special guests, without telling them about Raj and Sharmila.

After lunch we decided to take them shopping. We took them to our car and as I opened the door for them to get in, Mohan asked, "Whose car is this?" I answered that it belonged to me. I could see the surprise in their eyes as they got in the car, and I drove away to the store where we bought clothes for them. We then went to the market at Port Mourant where we bought some of my favorite fruits that I did not have since I left Guiana. We also bought some vegetables and fishes which brought back memories while I was growing up in Guiana.

The next few days before my big event, I traveled around the country meeting and inviting old friends, and I managed to get my old classmate friend Eva's address from her parents and I visited her. I was surprised that she recognized me after about eighteen years, and she was also surprised to see me. I introduced Monica as my wife, and she was happy in meeting both of us.

We spent about an hour catching up on old times as she told Monica about the good things that she heard about her from me when we were classmates. I asked Eva if she knew where Monica's sister, Chandra lived. She said she did not know her address, but she met her and was told that she lived at Skeldon and is a teacher at the Primary School. We then invited Eva to our reception and thanked her before leaving.

The following day Sharda traveled to Skeldon and promised us that she would get Chandra's address. She went to the school where Chandra worked and waited until she came out to go home after school was dismissed. Sharda approached her and both were happy in seeing each other. They hugged and Chandra invited Sharda to her home which was just a block from the school. Sharda replied that she would visit her the following day, which was Saturday. Chandra then gave Sharda her address and asked her to bring her family over, to which Sharda replied, "I would bring Jayboy and if it is ok with you, I would also bring two close friends." Chandra said it was ok. Both of them hugged each other as Sharda said "See you on tomorrow."

Monica was very happy that Sharda got her sister, Chandra's address and she was looking forward to be reunited with her after about eighteen years.

The following morning, Monica and I went shopping to buy gifts for Chandra and her family. We later picked up Jayboy and Sharda before heading to Chandra's house, which was about twenty miles away.

Upon reaching our destination, I stayed in the car while Sharda, Monica, and Jayboy proceeded to Chandra's house. Sharda and Jayboy went up the stairs and knocked on the door while Monica waited downstairs. Chandra opened the door, greeted her guests, and took them in the house.

Chandra then asked, "Where are your friends that you promised to bring."

Sharda replied "She is downstairs and will be up in a minute." Then at that moment there was a knock on the door. Sharda said. "My friend is here."

Chandra opened the door, she screamed "Monica! Is that you?" as she stared at her sister in disbelief.

Monica replied "Yes." as tears of joy flowed from her eyes as she and Chandra hugged each other. With tears still in her eyes Chandra told Monica how much she had missed her for the past eighteen years because they lost contact with each other.

Monica then told her, "I came back to Guiana a year after I departed to the United States looking for Ricky and because I was so disappointed and depressed I did not visit anyone."

Chandra said to Monica, "I am sorry to hear about Ricky's death," and she expressed her sympathy. She then continued to say that she was happy to hear that Monica did not marry Sugrim, the boy of her parents' choice and asked her whether she ever got married again.

Monica replied "Yes, I got married legally about two months   ago to the man whom I am madly in love with. I am in Guiana for
our wedding reception and I am here to invite you and your family for this special occasion."

Chandra then said, "I am dying to meet the man who stole my sister's heart."

Monica answered, "You already met him when he was a young boy growing up in Guiana."

At that moment I came up the stairs standing in front the door as Monica said, "Meet my husband."

Chandra stared at me and said, "He resembled Ricky, but he is dead."

Monica then told her "Ricky is not dead but is standing right in front of you. I waited eighteen years, praying and hoping that Ricky would some day reunite with me. I knew deep down in my heart that he was alive when everyone believed him to be dead and god had answered my prayers."

Chandra then hugged me with tears still in her eyes as she led me in the house and introduced me to her husband and her two children. We spent a wonderful day catching up as I told Chandra about my journey to Trinidad, meeting my uncle and finally my journey to United States where I met, and reunited with Monica.

Chandra also told us about her experience with her parents when they found out that she was in love with her now husband, Mark. Her parents wanted to do the same as they did with Monica, trying to get her married to someone of their choice. Chandra said she had no choice but to elope with Mark. Her parents could not do anything because she was not under age as was Monica. She said she never visited or saw her parents again.

I asked Chandra if she knew where her brother lived, and she replied that she did. He lived in Georgetown and was still working with the Ministry of Education. I then asked Chandra to accompany us the following day to Georgetown so that we could meet her brother. She agreed to go with us and I arranged that I will pick her up five in the morning so that we can catch the first ferry across the Berbice River to get to Georgetown.

We then had a delicious dinner of curry lamb and rice with Chandra's family before leaving for our homeward journey.

The following morning Jayboy, Sharda, Monica, and I traveled back to Skeldon where we picked up Chandra and headed on our journey to Georgetown. We boarded the ferry in my car at the New Amsterdam stelling to cross the Berbice River.

After about twenty minutes later, we reached Rosignal Stelling, the other side of the river. We then continued our journey through on West Berbice and East Coast Demerara, enjoying the scenery as I drove on the brick roads. I was wondering whether Monica's brother (Ron) was home and what would be his re-action towards us. We reached Georgetown four hours later and proceeded to Campbellville where Monica's brother lived.

As we reached our destination and stopped in-front Ron's house, I saw him in his yard watering his plants. Upon seeing the car stopped, Ron stared inquiringly as he walked towards the gate. Chandra then stepped out of the car and walked towards her brother and hugged him. He was surprised to see Chandra because that was the first time the two of them had met after she eloped and was disowned by the family. She was surprised to hear that Ron replied. "I missed you very much and I am very happy to see you. Who else is in the car? Please tell them to come in."

Chandra answered that Jayboy, Sharda and Monica along with her husband are in the car. Ron was shocked that Monica was in Guiana, and he said, "I am dying to meet her." He then walked to the car and called out to Monica. As soon as she got out of the car, Ron hugged her and told her how much he missed her.

He then looked in the car and saw me and said "Is that you, Ricky?"

I replied, "Yes." I could see the shocked expression on his face as he gazed at me and asked me to please come in. As soon as I came out the car, he hugged me and said that he was happy that I was alive and he was happy that Monica and I are back together again. He apologized for not standing up to his parents for separating us and wished he had done a lot more.

Ron once again invited us to come inside the house, which we did and he introduced us to his wife and son. We then chatted over breakfast, which was prepared by Ron's wife and Chandra. One of the main questions Ron had for me was about my whereabouts, when everyone thought that I was dead.

I told him about my journey to Trinidad where I found my uncle, then my journey to United States where I found Monica after eighteen years, and we were legally married. I then told him that we were there to invite him and his family to our wedding reception. To which he promised that they would surely attend this special occasion.

After spending a wonderful evening with Ron and his family, we decided that it was time for us to head back home before darkness fell upon us. So we bade farewell and headed to our car accompanied by Ron. He once again reiterated his disappointment that he did not do enough to keep us together and asked for our forgiveness which we accepted before we departed.

It was already dark when we dropped off Chandra at her home. She asked us to spend the night at her house, but we declined because the following morning she had to wake up early to go to work and we wanted to sleep in late. We promised her that we would spend a night with her before we leave Guiana. We then thanked her for accompanying us to Georgetown before heading home.

Two weeks before the big day approached, Raj and Sharmila came to Guiana. I went to pick them up at the airport. They were all excited to be in Guiana. Sharmila was very happy to be in the birth country of her parents and meeting family members that she never knew she had. Three days prior to the celebration, Ramoutar, Sita and all our families arrived from India. Ramoutar and Rukmin were emotional to be in the country where their brother was taken after they were separated.

After arriving home, Ramoutar told us, "This is the happiest day in my life, not only to be present at the wedding reception but also to be in the house where my brother lived and died." He said that he wished that he could have reunited with his brother and his family before his death so that he could repay him for all the good things his family did for him, from the time he was a struggling child living in poverty, before he moved in with my dad's family. They made him to be a special child and he owed everything he has today to my dad, Ramessar and his family.

Ramoutar, Rukmin, Ratnie, Mohabir and their children toured the rest of the house before going to the verandah, and Ramoutar sat on the rocking chair relaxing and enjoying the view outside as passers-by waved and greeted him. I later introduced Sharda, Jayboy and their children. Sita was very happy to meet the family that rescued me and did so many good things for me during my childhood and teenage years.

Sharda was very anxious to meet Sharmila because she was the only one in Guiana who knew that Monica had a daughter. Raj and Sharmila were also happy to meet Sharda's children, and they started to hangout together.

The following morning, which was a Saturday, Chandra and her family arrived just before Monica's brother, Ron and his family. They were introduced to Ram, and Sita and my guests from India. Raj and Sharmila were not at home at the time because they went out with Sharda's children.

Around 11:30 that morning, I saw Monica's parents (Mohan and Anjee) walking towards our house. I knew this would be my opportunity to reunite them with all their children and grand children. I went downstairs to meet them as they walked into my yard, and I escorted them upstairs. It was an emotional moment as Mohan and Anjee saw all their children together. They asked their children for forgiveness and told them how much they missed them. They were forgiven, and it was a joyous moment as they hugged each other.

Later, Raj, Sharmila and Sharda's children came back from their tour of the Village; and as Sharmila walked into the room where everyone had gathered, Chandra, Ron and their parents could not stop staring at her in astonishment. Chandra then pointed at Sharmila and asked, "Monica, this girl is an identical picture of you. She has to be your daughter". She then turned to Monica and questioned, "You never told us that you have a child?"

"Yes, she is my daughter, Sharmila" Monica answered.

They looked at each other baffled which prompted Chandra to ask. "You and Ricky reunited only a few months ago. Who is Sharmila's father? Did you remarry someone else after separating from Ricky?"

Monica smiled and replied, "Ricky is the only one I ever loved and I would never marry anyone else. Ricky is the father of Sharmila." She went on to tell her about her pregnancy with my child prior to leaving Guiana.

Monica then introduced Sharmila to her grandparents, to her uncle Ron, and his family and her Aunt, Chandra family. I could see tears of joy flowing from everyone eyes as they hugged Sharmila.

I was overcome with emotion seeing the happiness on Sharmila's face as she united with her newly found family members. The family she always dreamt of having but could not question her mom about, because she knew that it was a topic that her mom never wanted to discuss.

After Sharmila united with her cousins, she told them that it was time for them to know each other better, so she took them, along with Raj and Sharda's children to a nearby restaurant to celebrate. After spending an enjoyable time together, Sharmila, Raj and Jayboy went to the airport to pick up Jessica.

This was Jessica's first time to Guiana. She was born and raised in United States where she was deeply involved in the church, doing charitable work in her country. She was never married and she became a nun. Monica was very happy to see Jessica when she arrived at our house. She introduced her as her second mother and the godmother of Sharmila. Sita was also happy in meeting her after many years.

As evening approached, some of the neighbors and Sharda's friends came over to help with the preparation of foodstuff for the following day. They did all the cutting and chipping of the vegetables, getting them ready for the following morning's cooking while some men built a huge tent at the side of our house.

As night approached, instead of lighting the hand-lamps, Jayboy lit the gas lamps that I shipped to Guiana. He made arrangements with some of his musician friends who brought over their stereo system and played some wonderful songs as they danced until late in the night. They also played the tassa drums, which brought back memories of my teenage life. Ram and Mohabir also enjoyed the tassa music and Ram even tried playing one of his favorite tunes, which he said he played as a young boy in India. I was overjoyed to see how happy Ram was, as he was having such an enjoyable time until midnight when he decided that it was time for us to go to bed because we had to wake early in the morning to do the cooking for our celebration.

Around four the following morning of my big day, Jayboy, Sharda and some of their friends started the cooking. By the time I got out of bed around seven that morning the food was almost completely cooked. Sharda, Sita and Chandra were already making preparations for the religious ceremony as Monica and I had our breakfast with Mohabir, Ratnie, Rukmin and their children then we got ready for marriage ceremony.

Neighbors and friends started to arrive around eleven that morning and the priest arrived by eleven-thirty. The ceremony started around twelve. I could not resist looking at Monica in her beautiful sari. I complimented her on her beauty as she complimented me on my Indian outfit. We sat under a tent that was built with bamboo posts, covered with coconut branches. It was well decorated with balloons and colored ribbons rapped around the posts and hung under the tent. We sat under the center of the tent where a well-decorated bamboo post was placed and the religious items were set-up.

The ceremony was not the normal Indian wedding because we had already completed the formal ceremony when we eloped eighteen years ago. It was more of a renewing our vows and a type of wedding known by the Indians as *Jaimal wedding*. The priest was the same one that was in charge of the Mandir (church) where Monica and I attended when we were kids. He knew my father very well and he even talked highly of him during the ceremony.

Ram and Rukmin performed the father and mother's roles for me and Mohan, and Anjee performed the father and mother roles for Monica. The most touching moment was when Mohan handed over his daughter, Monica, to me and he once again apologized for not doing this eighteen years ago. He asked Ram and Rukmin for forgiveness as they hugged each other. Mohan then looked up above, raised his hand and said; "Ramessar I know your spirit is looking down on us today on this special occasion. I ask of you to please forgive me for all the wrong things I did to you and family. I wish I had done this eighteen years ago in your presence. Please forgive me."

During the ceremony we once again took the seven steps around the fire and the renewal of our vows after each step. We exchanged rings and garlands made of beautiful, scented Jasmine flowers. At the end of the ceremony, Ram gave a touching speech talking about my dad and expressed his happiness to be in the house of his brother to witness and be a part of the marriage of his son. He thanked everyone that helped me during my struggling days and made special mention of Sharda and Jayboy. I also thanked Ram for being there as a father for me and for giving me everything that I have today.

I then introduced Sharmila as the daughter of Monica and me to the audience. Most people were shocked and astonished because they heard that I met Monica a few months ago after our separation for eighteen years; and at the time Monica and I were together, we did not have any children. Before anyone asked a question I told them that when Monica and I were separated, she was pregnant with my child who happened to be Sharmila. They all were happy to hear the good news.

After the ceremony was completed, the music started as everyone had delicious Indian foods on special leaves known as *Purine leaves* (Lotus flower leaves). I enjoyed eating the *guruma* (mango jam) with *puri rotie* (white pita bread cooked in ghee.)

After everyone finished their meals, Monica and I greeted our friends. I was happy meeting my high school friends, Peter, Mahadeo, Rohit and Eva and her family. We all had a wonderful evening as everyone danced to the tune of Indian hit songs and tassa drum music until late in the night.

I invited all our family and friends for a family get together the following day. Ram also included the aged and poor Villagers. He gave them food and gifts of clothing and money on behalf of my father. The rest of the day we enjoyed celebrating with family and friends. I was very happy to be amongst all my living family members and all the people that were in my life during the different periods while I was growing up. Sharmila and Raj enjoyed every moment with their new-found family. They spent most of their times with their nieces, nephews, cousins and also Sharda's children.

Two days after spending a wonderful time reuniting with all my family members, Ram, Raj, Sharmila Sita and my Indian guests departed to Trinidad and Jessica left for United States. Monica and I stayed in Guiana for the rest of the week and continued spending time with our old as well as new friends. During the day I visited places of interest that I spent during my early life. In the evenings I sat on my rocking chair in my verandah enjoying the view and sometimes reflected on my life while growing up in Guiana.

One day in particular when Monica and Sharda went to the market, I was gazing at the horizon from my verandah as I started to reflect on the days as a young boy in Guiana. Many bushes were around the lawns and street corners and small puddles of water were the breathing ground for mosquitoes. I remembered being stung by swarms of mosquitoes as they came by the thousands when I went to the backyards.

My dad burned coconut husk and shells to keep them away when we gathered outside during the nights. Indoor we lit mosquito coils to keep away the few that made their way into the house. We inhaled the mosquito coils smoke along with the black smoke coming from the bottle lamps that were used for light.

I remember every morning waking up to the fowl cock crowing, the chirping of birds and the barking of dogs. That was our alarm clock because we did not have any clocks. We also looked at our shadows on sunny days to get the time of the day.

I remember after breakfast each day my task was to sweep the floors of our house, then under the house using a broom made of stems from the coconut branches. Once weekly, I washed and scrubbed the floors in the house using a metal scraper instead of a brush, which made the floor look as new as when it was first installed. I fetched buckets of water from the canals for both drinking and washing. I carried the bucket filled with water on my head and emptied it into a large drum. I also bathed daily at the canals and on weekends swam with friends.

I remember going to the farm or seashore with a cutlass to cut wood for cooking. I tied logs in bundles and carried the bundles on my head. At home I cut the wood into small pieces and left them to dry, then used them for cooking in our wood stove called a *fireside*.

I remember most of my early life, walking barefooted. I even went to school without any shoes. The roads were all dirt roads. There were no brick roads, and when it rained, the mud and clay stuck on my feet as if I had shoes on them. I had to scrape and wash the mud off before going into the house.

Some of the most enjoyable times I had were when I went donkey riding at the playground or at the pasture. I was also happy playing softball and cricket. I used bats that were made of coconut branches. I enjoyed catching fish with hooks as well as nets and some times with my bare hands. I had fun in the cane fields catching *hassa* (a kind of catfish) with my hand during nesting seasons using *blacksage* leaves that were rubbed onto the palm of my hand to attract the fish into my hand; and sometimes I got eggs under the nests. I also loved eating sugar canes while in the fields peeling off the skins with my teeth or a cutlass.

I enjoyed drinking mauby drinks and eating sweet cakes and cassava bread on special occasions and on holidays, having lamb or chicken curry. I was happy when my dad cooked the cook-up rice, rotie, fish curry and fried fish. I enjoyed eating green mangoes. I peeled the mangoes, cut them up in small pieces, mixed them with salt and pepper and had them as snacks. I also had tamarind with salt and pepper. I enjoyed eating the Jamoon fruit mixed with salt and pepper.

As I looked at the tall coconut trees, the leaves were swaying as the wind blew against them. I remembered climbing those high trees without any ropes, picking dried coconuts to make coconut chutney and oil as well as water coconut which I drank to quench my thirst. I also climbed the mango trees, hanging on the small limb as I tried to get the ripened mangoes. I love the black spice and long mango varieties.

While growing up, there were no radios, no television, no telephone, and no cars. Our main means of transportation was by donkey carts or cow carts. Everyone was accustomed to walking long distances to and from their destinations. Later during my teenage life, I managed to get a bicycle, which was my main means of transportation.

During the holidays, I enjoyed Christmas when men from neighboring village dressed as *longladies*, wearing long dresses with stilts on their feet, danced with other dancers to the beat of drums and calypso songs. I also had fun on Easter when I flew my kite with other friends competing to find out whose kite went the highest and whose kite made the loudest singing sound. I also had fun in celebrating two Hindu festivals. *Pagwah* which is a celebration of welcoming spring and giving thanks to god for a good crop.

We celebrated it by going to church spraying colored water or colored powder on each other and eating special sweet dishes. *Diwalie,* the other Hindu holiday, is a festival of "good over evil" by lighting little lamps called *dyas.*

As I started to remember the happy days Monica and I spent as children, someone tapped my shoulder awakening me from my deep thoughts. I turned around and saw Monica standing behind me. She just returned from the market with Sharda. She bought me some ginnips, sapodillas and star apples which were some of my favorite fruits as a young boy. She sat beside me as we enjoyed snacking on the delicious fruits.

As weekend approached, it was time for us to say goodbye to our family and friends. Jayboy and Sharda accompanied us to the airport, and we enjoyed the last couple of hours with them before departing to Trinidad.

We spent a few days with Ram, Sita, my aunt Rukmin, her children, Mohabir, Ratnie and their children. I took them site seeing before Mohabir and his family departed to India.
Ram asked Rukmin and her two sons, Sewkumar and Narine with their families, to stay in Trinidad. They accepted and Sewkumar and Narine helped us manage the cattle ranch and rice industry. They stayed at our cottage house with their families and Rukmin stayed at our house in Trinidad. Four weeks later I joined Raj and Sharmila in United States. Both of them were working part time with our Business, and I was very happy that they were learning all aspects of our operation.

As years went by, Raj and Sharmila graduated from College and started working full time. Monica and I had more time to travel between Trinidad and United States, spending more time in Trinidad, taking care of our business as well as spending more time with Ram, Rukmin and Sita. Monica and I also visited Guiana more frequently, enjoying some vacation time in our birth country with our friends and family.

Raj and Sharmila also spent most holidays at our house in Guiana with their newly found family and friends. They had no problems traveling around because they had a car that was left for them to use while they were in Guiana.

Chapter 22
Conclusion

During my lifetime, I was faced with many challenging experiences and loves that came in different forms. Throughout these experiences, I was hurt so many times that I concluded that it was normal to feel hurt. I learned to cope with hurtful love, as I experienced many times when I was separated from the ones that I truly loved. I also experienced love that caused me to have an unexplainable happiness that none other could replace, as those happy days I spent with my childhood girl friend and surrounded by wonderful friends and family.

I also experienced unexplained things that love could make a person do. Things that I never thought I was capable of doing. I learned that love can bring out the worst or best in a person; even facing death for the ones I truly love. During my life, I also learned to face life by separating true love apart from lust, as I did with Monica and Rose. I also learned to respect the love for family which I cherished with my parents, Ram, Sita, Raj and Sharmila.

The most important lesson that I learned during my life time is to never give up hope, although at times I felt that life was not worth living. I tried to think in a positive way as if I was just going through a passing phase that would not last forever. I always strived for betterment; and I knew deep down in my heart that if I tried hard, some day I would be a better person and my dreams will come through. I never gave up hope, although I experienced many tragedies, and at the end I achieved everything that I wanted in life.

I have come to believe that life is what you want to make it. If you have a dream, you should go for it; nothing is impossible. I came a long way, and the dreams that I had, which I often thought were impossible to achieve, have come true. Growing up in Guiana, struggling each day to survive, I never expected that God would guide me and help me to fulfill my dreams from rags to riches.

I learned that Life is what we want to make of it. There are many paths we'll face, some good and some bad. If we follow the path towards our dreams, we will achieve them even if, at times, we will feel that they are impossible to achieve, as I did. With determination, hope, faith and God's blessings, we will achieve our goals. Shoot for it. Nothing is impossible.

www.ingramcontent.com/pod-product-compliance
Lightning Source LLC
Chambersburg PA
CBHW050553300426
44112CB00013B/1894